PRACTICAL MAGIC
for Beginners

About the Author

Brandy Williams is a Wiccan high priestess and ceremonial magician. She has been practicing and teaching magic for over twenty-five years. She is also a scholar, musician, and artist.

PRACTICAL MAGIC
for Beginners

*Techniques
&
Rituals
to Focus
Magical Energy*

Brandy Williams

Llewellyn Publications
St. Paul, Minnesota

First Edition
First Printing, 2005

Book design and editing by Joanna Willis
Cover design by Ellen Dahl
Cover photograph © 2004 by Doug Deutscher
Illustrations on pages 59, 82, and 128 by Llewellyn art department

Library of Congress Cataloging-in-Publication Data
Williams, Brandy, 1956–
   Practical magic for beginners: techniques & rituals to focus
magical energy / Brandy Williams.
      p.   cm.
   Includes bibliographical references and index.
   ISBN 0-7387-0661-2
   1. Magic. 2. Ritual. I. Title.

BF1611.W744 2005
133.4'3—dc22

                                        2004057744

Llewellyn Publications
A Division of Llewellyn Worldwide, Ltd.
P.O. Box 64383, Dept. 0-7387-0661-2
St. Paul, MN 55164-0383, U.S.A.
www.llewellyn.com

Printed in the United States of America

Other Books in the For Beginners Series

Astrology for Beginners
William W. Hewitt

Chakras for Beginners
David Pond

Divination for Beginners
Scott Cunningham

Healing Alternatives for Beginners
Kay Henrion

Magick for Beginners
J. H. Brennan

Meditation for Beginners
Stephanie Clement

Psychic Development for Beginners
William W. Hewitt

To Theodore Gill,
my most faithful coteacher,
reader, supporter, and love.

Contents

CONTENTS

Exercises

Chapter 1

Chapter 2

Chapter 3

Chapter 4

Chapter 5

Chapter 6

Chapter 7

Chapter 8

Chapter 9

Chapter 11

Chapter 12

Introduction

Introduction to Practical Magic

Magic is the art of the possible. Understanding what magic is, and how to use it, gives us the invaluable power of choice. We can decide where we want to live, how we work, the kind of love we want to invite into our lives. Magic can give us the freedom and the knowledge to follow a spiritual path.

The power of choice doesn't come about simply by knowing the right spell. While spellcraft is a venerable branch of magic with much useful knowledge to offer, simply putting the right ingredients together and saying a rhyming couplet will not necessarily achieve the result we want. For reliable results we must possess the skills to make the spell happen. To acquire those skills, we need to exercise them and flex our magical muscles. We must also understand why it is that magic works and what processes underlie the actions that we take to affect the world.

When we first exercise magical skills, change happens very quickly. The smallest action has immediate positive results. This is because our culture has neglected magic for many centuries. We've lost the day-to-day contact with the energies of the earth, the planets, and our own minds, the connections that make us aware of the processes that shape the world. Magic puts us in touch with those energies once again. As we continue to develop magical skills, we lay the foundation for more complicated ritual actions. While we are doing magic to improve our lives, we find that our lives have become more magical. We are shaping ourselves in order to shape the world.

Many religions and philosophies use some kind of magic in their spiritual practice. Today, magic has fallen out of favor among most Christians, although in Hellenistic times Christians used spells alongside Jews and Pagans. This book does not care whether you are Christian, Wiccan, Pagan, Buddhist, Hindu, Muslim, or atheist; whether you are a Mason or a Rosicrucian or a Theosophist; whether you are black or white or multicolored, male or female or transitioning, young or old. Magic is for everyone. You can combine the techniques you will learn in this book with any religious or philosophical system, or use them on their own.

In this book we will be learning a vocabulary: What is energy? What exactly does it mean to ground? What is a ward? We will learn basic techniques of protection, for ourselves and for our possessions. We will learn how to cleanse ourselves and our homes of energies we don't want around, and how to attract the energies we do want. We will look at the effect of time on rituals. We will examine magical processes underlying spells and what makes rites actually work. We will learn a ritual methodology that allows us to put together our own rites. Finally, we'll talk about the results we want from our rites, and look at some examples of created rituals designed to achieve specific, real-world results.

This book is short on theory and long on practice. From the first chapter we jump into exercises that put the lesson into use. Later, you can fit these lessons into any religious, philosophical, or magical system that you like, and any system will provide us with a great deal more theory about why ritual works the way it does. This book concentrates on techniques that are immediately practical.

Whatever path you are on, this book will give you the tools to straighten out your physical life, and provide a solid foundation for your spiritual pursuits. With the techniques of ritual magic, you can go on to study one of the branches of Witchcraft; ceremonial magic, including the Golden Dawn, Aurum Solis, and Thelemic systems; any of the Neopagan religious survivals and reconstructions; Gnostic Christianity; mystic Judaism; Sufism; or any religion or philosophy you choose. Or, you can simply use ritual magic as a way to organize your spellwork, and live a happier life. What you do with this power is up to you!

Practical magic describes the kind of magic that helps you to live your life the way you want to live. It also means that as you develop your skills, you see the world more and more as a magical place. It becomes easier and easier to see and use the processes that shape the world and your experience in it. Magic becomes the way you live.

Introduction to the Author

Whenever I read a book on magic, I am curious about the writer. Who is this person? What kind of experience does she have? Has he actually done the exercises he talks about, or is he running an experiment—on me? My favorite books are those that discuss the writers' experiences, and give stories about how the exercises worked for them.

So I'm going to give you a brief introduction to who I am. I've had a diverse magical career. In my late teens and early twenties, I studied several martial arts. I learned the 108 movements of a complete tai chi form. I took beginner's aikido, where I learned how to breathe and move energy in my body, and tae kwon do, where I learned how to dance with an opponent. I also studied a bit of yoga, which similarly focused on breathing and finding one's energy. This training affected my understanding of energy at least as profoundly as any of the formal magical disciplines.

I also studied psychological techniques. I read through Freud, Jung, and Adler, and the Neuro-Linguistic Programming studies of Bandler and Grinder. The NLP worldview affected me deeply, as it is imminently practical. It is focused on what the therapist can see, and how the senses work to represent the world. Keeping NLP in mind helps make sense out of the jumble of magical practices.

I spent my teen years trying to figure out what I believed. When I discovered Witchcraft I immediately felt that I had come home. "Once a Witch, always a Witch" was a saying in one of the books I read early on, and I felt that I was already a Witch. Later I found a traditional Wiccan line that was willing to initiate me. Wicca is still my first love as a religion.

I did a retreat in my late twenties, spending three years living and working in an apple orchard and studying ceremonial magic. I worked through the Golden Dawn knowledge lectures and all of the exercises in the Aurum Solis books. Later, I also studied the philosophy and religion of Thelema. After my Qabalah retreat, I moved back to a large city and became quite active in the Neopagan community, creating rituals and gatherings.

Both my Pagan reconstruction work and my ceremonial magic work led me to the study of history, which remains my enduring passion. I discovered that the basics of today's occult sciences rest in a series of ideas and rituals collected in the Hermetica and in the Greek magical papyri. For example, the idea of four directions, four winds, and four archangels are all found in these documents, which are two millennia old. The Hellenistic culture that produced these texts mixed Christian, Jewish, Greek, Babylonian, and Egyptian sources. These magical ideas and techniques spread widely around the world. Hindu texts talk about the four directions, and the Islamic Arabic world absorbed a good many Hermetic doctrines.

I have taught with a rotating crew of several other teachers in a series of classes we jointly named "School of Night." Our most popular class was an eight-week course in magical fundamentals. For these classes I drew on all my experiences in martial arts, psychology, Witchcraft, ceremonial magic, Thelema, group ritual construction, and history to put together a pared-down set of techniques that could be simply learned by anyone with a desire to explore magic. Today I continue to teach classes in magic both to beginners and experienced practitioners, to Wiccans, Pagans, and ceremonial magicians, and anyone who is interested in learning about the occult arts.

This book comes out of those classes. I hasten to add that while I have at times taught with others, I take total responsibility for the material in this book—both its virtues and its flaws. People continually ask me to provide them with written material to augment the classes I give. I needed a text I could hand to people and say, "Here—this should get you started!"

However much I study, I realize that I am still just a beginner in the magical sciences. There is so much to learn, so many avenues to explore, that it can easily occupy an entire happy lifetime. I hope to continue to learn and grow for many years to come.

The exercises and rites in this book are not just for beginners. I come back to them again and again. This is the stuff I use day to day: ground, center, shield, ward my house and my car, work small rites for friendship and love and prosperity. These are fundamental skills not because you learn them and forget them, or learn them and go on to bigger and better things, but because they are the skills that you use over and over every day of your magical life.

one

Moving Energy

Every ritual—in fact, every magical act—we perform relies on our ability to move energy through our bodies. Understanding energy is the key to understanding how to work magic. It's the word we hear most often when people talk about magic, and it's the least well defined. Mostly we learn what the word means from context—how people talk about energy.

The word *energy* means something different to a scientist. If you know the scientific definitions of the word, it's very tempting to use them to explain magical energy, so it's important to keep in mind that they're not the same. The scientific understanding of energy is at best a metaphor for magical energy; if you lean too much on the hard science definitions, you run the risk of limiting your understanding of how energy works in the occult sciences.

In daily life we talk about the energy that makes electricity, which runs the house at the flip of a switch. Companies buy and sell this type of energy as a commodity. We also talk about physical energy (our ability to move around, whether we are tired or fresh and relaxed) and emotional energy (whether we are depressed or excited and raring to go!).

In magical terms, energy means something different from all of these definitions. It is a power that we cannot measure with an instrument. Magicians talk about an energy body, which can circulate and store energy. There is also the energy of the forces around us: the elements of fire and wind and water, the planet earth, and the other planets in our solar system. We understand the energy of these forces and how they interlace within our world.

Energy constantly moves in your body. You can attract energy from other sources, and circulate it inside yourself. You can also use your body to move energy around in ritual space. In this chapter we will be focusing on how your personal energy interacts with the energy of your environment, and how to control that interaction consciously.

The body comes equipped with its own human energy. Martial artists sometimes call this energy *chi* or *ki*. You can feel it very easily just by raising your hands.

FEELING ENERGY

Lift your arms to chest level and turn your hands so that the palms face each other. Hold them there for a moment or so. You have set up an energy connection between your hands. What do you experience? Do you see the energy, or feel it? Give yourself a moment to notice your reaction before you read on.

It's okay if you don't feel anything; it can take some time to become aware of chi. People often describe the feeling of energy flowing between their hands as tingly or warm. You might have even found that your hands started to heat up and felt a pressure against your palms. People usually use physical analogues to describe energy: color or brightness (red or yellow, dull or bright), texture or temperature (smooth or rough, hot or cool), and pitch or volume (high or low, loud or soft).

Just as the physical body has organs and blood vessels, the energy body has *chakras* (centers of energy) and *meridians* (channels of energy). The energy or subtle body also has a skin: the *aura*. Energy is constantly circulating within your energy body. We take it in and give it off, use it up in activity and replenish it.

Health is essential to the practice of ritual magic. If the physical body is trashed, the energy body is going to be trashed too. That doesn't mean you can't do these exercises—you can. Start circulating energy now, and that will start to clear up the physical body too. Just follow up with better health habits!

It is also important to pay attention to the health of the energy body. You can damage your energy body just as you can damage your physical body. Circulating energy helps to keep the channels clear and flowing freely, and protecting the chakras helps to keep them from knotting up or losing energy.

Most energy work involves the central column. This is a pathway through the center of the body from the head to the feet. Centers of energy, or chakras, are located along the central column. The energy body meridians extend from the central column and branch out along your arms and legs. There are also energy centers that give out and take in energy in the palms of your hands and the soles of your feet. (See Figure 2 in chapter 7.)

We don't normally notice the pumping of the heart, and most of the time we aren't conscious of the process of breathing. In the same way, the energy circulation in the energy body goes on at a level below conscious awareness. We can become conscious of energy, just as we can become conscious of our heartbeat. In fact, noticing our heartbeat and breathing is a good way to begin learning about energy.

CONSCIOUS BREATHING

Sit in a comfortable chair or cross-legged on the floor. Find your pulse by touching your wrist or any other place you can find a heartbeat. Now breathe in for four heartbeats, hold your breath for two heartbeats, breathe out for four heartbeats, and hold your exhalation for two heartbeats. Do this four times.

This can feel pretty strange the first time you do it. You might find that your heartbeat slows down. That's okay, just keep on counting. You might find that you're breathing very quickly or slowly, depending on how fast your heart is beating. If you breathe slowly you take in a lot of oxygen, which might cause a little dizziness. All of these effects go away with practice.

Many ritual techniques assume that we are able to control our own breathing. We can use our breath to pull a particular kind of energy into the body. We might use rhythmic breathing to time a given operation. As air is vitally necessary to our continuing ability to walk around on the planet, it can become a carrier for the more subtle energies we will work with.

Our personal energy exists within the field of energy of the earth and it interacts with the earth's energy. Just as we are constantly taking in physical energy from the air we breathe, the water we drink, the food we eat, and the sunshine on our skin, so is our energy body constantly taking in and giving out energy from the forces all around us.

The body's energy is especially linked to the energy of the earth and the sun. All of us move around within the energy field of the earth. We sometimes think of ourselves as walking on the earth, but in truth we are walking around inside the earth, as we are moving within an atmosphere that extends many miles above us. The earth's energy surrounds us—below, above, and all around—and sustains us throughout our lives.

We can learn to consciously direct the energy of the earth into our bodies. This serves as an immediate source of energy when we're tired. Similarly, we can learn to take excess energy from our bodies. Some people refer to this exercise as *grounding*. The idea of grounding is to balance the state of your energy body with the charge in the earth's energy around you. If we're low on energy, we can take some from the earth, and if we have a lot of energy and it's making us jittery, we can put the extra back into the ground.

TOUCHING THE EARTH: THE MOUNTAIN

Take your shoes and socks off and stand on the floor. If you can go outside, it's great to do this exercise on the bare earth. Feel and see energy moving from the earth through the soles of your feet, into your body, all the way up your legs, up your central column, to the top of your head. Now push the energy from the top of your head back down the central column, through your legs, and into the earth.

Grounding is half of the process of grounding and centering. *Centering* means finding out where the energy is in your body, and starting every body and energy movement from a sense of calm and power.

The easiest way to center is to focus on a part of the body that martial artists call the *one point* or *tan t'ien*. This is a point in the abdomen about two fingers' width below the belly button. It's the center of gravity in the body, the point of physical balance. The one point is a very convenient place to start and end energy circulations.

FINDING THE CENTER

Stand with your feet about a shoulder's width apart. Bend your knees slightly. Place your attention at your one point. Now rock forward and back. Let the rocking get smaller and smaller until you balance and stop. Next, rock from side to side. Let the rocking get smaller and smaller until you find your center of balance, and stop naturally.

We can move energy into and out from the body through the soles of the feet. We can also give out and take in energy through the top of the head. The Tree exercise trains us to draw energy from the earth and circulate it. It also helps to cleanse and balance the energy body.

THE TREE

Feel and see energy moving out like roots from your one point, down through your legs, to the soles of your feet. Now push those roots down into the ground. Keep pushing down, as far as you can go, until you feel your roots coming to a natural stop.

When you have reached your comfortable depth, see and feel energy moving up through your roots, through the soles of your feet, and into your one point.

Next, feel and see the energy moving up your central column, to the top of your head, and then a little bit beyond to a chakra or globe a few inches above your head. Let the energy spill out from that center and shower down all around you back into the earth.

You are circulating earth energy up through your roots, out the top of your head, and back through your roots again.

When you have finished, let the energy fall back down the central column to your one point. Gradually feel and see your roots ascending back through the earth, through the soles of your feet, and back into your one point.

We naturally draw energy from the earth. Like all other living things, we also draw energy from the sun, and to a lesser extent from the moon. We can also learn to consciously circulate solar and lunar energy through the energy body.

Sun and Moon

Stand where you can see the sun or moon. It's nice if the light can be touching your skin but not necessary. Now see and feel the energy center just above your head. See and feel the moonlight or sunlight entering that center. Draw it down through the central column to your one point. From there, push the energy out along your arms and along your legs. Feel it filling up your body.

When you have finished, let the energy move down your legs through the soles of your feet and into the earth.

Once we have filled ourselves with energy, we can use it in a magical working or we can push it back down into the earth. We do not return solar and lunar energy by pushing it up out the central column back toward the sky. Whenever we have generated more energy than we can use in an energy exercise, the best thing to do with it is to push it back down into the earth. There are two reasons for this. First, moving energy down the central column is safest for the human body, as it tends to balance and calm your energy. Also, the human energy body is more attuned to the energy of the earth, and belongs to the earth's field. We can pull energy in from the planets, but it is much harder to exchange energy and give it back—it will still be moving through the earth's field. So to ground excess energy, we put it down into the earth.

With the exercises in this chapter we have begun to take conscious control of the energy body. In the next few chapters we will study the senses of sight and hearing, movement, and learn to work more effectively in the magical world.

two

Expanding the Senses

The practice of magic involves different kinds of sensing. All of us learned over the course of childhood that the real world is composed of physical objects that can be measured, tested, and universally acknowledged. When your friends gather around a table, everybody agrees that the table exists. We all learned that we have five senses, three of which are major and two minor: the sense of sight, hearing, and feeling, and the lesser-used senses of taste and smell.

We also learned that any other kind of sensing is imaginary. There are two worlds: the inner and the outer. In the outer world, everybody is sitting around the table. You can close your eyes and imagine yourself in Tahiti, but that is private to you, and not real.

The psychological worldview of Neuro-Linguistic Programming has terms to describe these two experiences:

uptime, which is sensing with your eyes, ears, and skin; and *downtime,* which is going inside yourself and making images, sounds, and feelings. This is a very useful understanding that we will come back to in detail.

Which type of sensing is considered legitimate varies depending on cultural fashion. At the turn of the century, the mechanistic worldview was so entrenched that psychological insights were dismissed. The psychological sciences fought long and hard for acceptance. Even now we tend to reject the validity of personal experience unless it can be externally measured and verified by an "objective" independent observer. If you experience something that others do not, it's not real.

The occult sciences made a similar bid for respect, setting up experiments and collating the results, hoping for acceptance into the larger scientific world. Today there are associations that continue this work, but by and large the psychological paradigm has absorbed magical understandings. If you see, hear, or feel something that your friends at the table do not, then you are making it up, and it has no external reality. This split of the world into the physical and the psychological is so hardened at this moment in time that few people remember the earlier understanding of the senses as expandable.

There are people who see, hear, and feel phenomena that are not measurable, and that not everyone can experience. The language that describes these senses is partly scientific, and partly ancient: *extrasensory perception, the supernatural, clairvoyance, mediumship,* and *seership.*

Probably the hardest thing you will be asked to do as a magician is to develop the ability to explore the senses beyond your physical senses. I'm not going to tell you that you have to jettison science's disbelief in these senses. I am going to say that if you act as if these senses exist, you will have some interesting and useful experiences.

There are two emotional blocks to developing psychic perception. The first is all those kid science programs that "debunk the supernatural." These tend to be strictly propaganda. They state a bald opinion and hold opposing viewpoints up to ridicule. The second is the somewhat deep-rooted idea that you have to be born with the talent—that some people have it, and some people don't.

In fact, magicians have been developing psychic skills for centuries. While some people will be better at it than others, everyone can develop enough psychic skill to be able to do effective ritual magic.

There is an interesting common understanding of psychic phenomenon that is hardly remarked upon. Almost everyone has had an experience at some point that is not explainable, and almost everyone knows someone who has had a premonition or visitation. For example, the man saw his father standing in the door, and later found out that was the moment he had died. The wife of the man taken hostage never gave up hope, because she knew that her husband was alive, and they were reunited after a decade. The man did not get on the plane because he had a terrible feeling, and the plane crashed and killed everyone on board.

Many psychic phenomena are associated with ghosts or with talking to spirits. The Spiritualist understanding of mediumship primarily focuses on talking to people who have died. There is another kind of mediumship that involves talking to spirits on other planes or other planets called *channeling* or *trance channeling*. Jane Roberts's Seth material is a good example of this.

In the following chapters we will explore each of these kinds of perception: using the external senses, tracing the working of the inner senses, and developing the psychic senses. We will be exploring each of these individually, but they do overlap. Some phenomenologists believe that there is a single sense that presents information about the world to our brains. The brain separates this information out into what we know as sight, sound, hearing, taste, and smell. However, it is at the root level of the single common sense that the psychic perception works.

The exploration of the senses we are about to embark upon is an example of the alchemical dictum *solve et coagula,* or "separate and combine." We will look at each of the senses in turn: external sight and visualization; external hearing and affirmation; external feeling and internal sensation; observation, inner experience, and expanded sensing. Then we will combine these newly developed skills again in ritual magic work.

Journals

The first magical exercise is to begin to make a record of the magical work we do. Magicians tend to keep several kinds of journals. Many magicians keep a daily diary, either privately or online. Keeping a daily diary is a memory aid. We might think we'll never forget this amazing moment, but then when we read a diary entry a year later, we discover how much we would have forgotten. A diary entry can remind us of details that we would otherwise forget.

Many magicians keep daily journals, but it's not a requirement. However, nearly all magicians keep a record of their magical workings. This serves as a check and balance to our work. If an operation succeeds, we know what we did right, and if it doesn't go as planned, we can check to see what went wrong. We might engage in a working that materializes quite a few years later, or that turned out to be the first in a long series of workings, and we'll want to know exactly what we did that first time.

When recording a working, note the date, including the year. It's very frustrating to find a yellowed scrap of paper marked "July 9." What year was that? Also note the time and the place. You might jot down the phase of the moon, and any unusual events, like a solar eclipse. You can always calculate moon phases and planetary positions later if you have the date, time, and place. You can make a lengthy entry, noting a lot of details, or just jot down the essentials: "Did Yesterday exercise. Couldn't remember what I had for lunch."

Journal

Get a plain spiral notebook. Record the results of one of the exercises in this book in the notebook. Now get a colored pen, and record the results of another exercise. Pick up a blank bound journal and use it to record an exercise. If you own a computer, try recording one of the exercises online.

Exploring different types of journals is fun, even if you've been journaling for a long time. A plain spiral notebook is a good type to start with because sometimes people are intimidated by the crisp, lovely look of the pages in a professionally bound blank book. Don't be shy—write on those pages! Fill them up. Write a list of colors, the days of the week, or the thought flitting across your mind at that exact instant.

In our magical life we will fill up many, many journals. I have two boxes filled with physical journals: three-ring binders with dividers, spiral notebooks, and piles of bound books in every shape and color. I have floppy disks filled with notes. I have online diaries that consist of many megs of data. As time goes on I find them increasingly valuable. There are operations I did while I was young that I would never ever have remembered if I didn't write them down!

With journals in hand, we are ready to begin our exploration of the magic of the senses. In the next three chapters we will explore magical sight, hearing, and feeling.

three

Sight

Magical practice involves new ways of seeing. In the course of performing a spell or ritual we will visualize the flow of energy. Learning to recognize what we see and how to visualize clearly helps rituals work toward the result we want.

Just as we observe the world with sight, sound, and feeling, so do we represent the world to ourselves with images, sounds and words, and internal feelings. We move back and forth between creating an internal world and observing the external world without being consciously aware of the transition. Our first task is to notice when our awareness shifts from the outside world to the world within. Then we can get really good at observing with eyes and ears and skin, and practice the skills involved in creating an interior world.

NOTICE THE WORLD: COLORS

Find a place where you can do this exercise comfortably. It can be in your own house, in your office, or commuting to work on a bus, train, or ferry. In your own house you might feel a little less self-conscious, but out in the world you have a lot more stimuli. Set a timer for one minute or put a clock in your field of vision. Now look around. How many colors do you see? Keep counting until the minute is up.

Did your mind wander during the exercise? Did you find yourself thinking about what you did for lunch, how upset you are with your boss, how happy you are that you get to see the movie tomorrow? Most people find it hard to concentrate for one minute, especially at first. I've done this exercise with hundreds of people, and none of them lasted longer than a minute the first time they did it.

One way to get better at concentration is to learn breathing exercises. Many disciplines, such as yoga, Buddhism, and martial arts, teach breathing exercises to quiet the mind. The following is my favorite.

QUIET THE MIND

Sit comfortably on the floor cross-legged or kneeling and sitting back on your heels. Focus your mind on your one point. Breathe in for a count of ten (you can use your heartbeat, or just count to ten). Hold your breath for a count of three. Now

exhale for a count of ten, and hold your breath for a
count of three. Repeat ten times.

The point of the exercise is to empty your mind and
focus only on your one point. During this exercise, thoughts
will almost certainly stir in your mind. If you lose your
count, pick up where you left off. If you keep your count but
find yourself thinking about something, as soon as you
notice the thought, bring your mind back to your one point.

This is probably the most difficult exercise in this entire
book. Very little in our schooling has prepared us to be this
still. You might have an aptitude for quiet, and hit the
mark immediately; or it might take you years to go all ten
breaths without a thought. Success isn't measured by how
long you can still your mind, but by the fact that you are
doing the exercise.

With a quieter mind, we can go back to observing the
world.

NOTICE THE WORLD: SHAPES

Set a timer for one minute, or put a clock in your
field of vision. Now look around. How many shapes
do you see? Keep counting until the minute is up.

When you look around for shapes, you are also giving
your mind something lively to focus on, so for most
people this exercise makes it a little easier to keep going for
the full minute without letting the mind wander. The difference between counting breaths and counting shapes is

that counting breaths is meditation, while counting shapes is concentration. Again, if you find your mind wandering, bring it back to the observation. For this exercise, the idea is to just notice exactly when you stop observing, and when you fall into your own internal world.

We use our eyes to see the world, and we use images to recreate the world. Images come in two major categories: those we remember and those we create.

VISUAL REMEMBERING
Think of a room in your house. If you're in your house now, it should not be the room you're in. What color is the floor? Where are the doors into the room? Where are the light switches?

VISUAL CONSTRUCTION
What would a lime-green giraffe look like? How about a pink horse?

These two exercises point out the difference between images that we remember and images that we create. We will come back to memory later. For now, we are interested in constructing images.

Many people believe that they cannot create images. In fact, if you have come this far in this book, you have proven that you can visualize—you've been visualizing many of these exercises, even if you didn't notice. Humans encode experience using sight, sound, and feelings; every memory captures the input of all the senses. However, most of us use one mode of perception, and are not conscious of the others. If you find it easy to make images, you probably find it harder to get in touch with what you feel. If you find it easy to feel, you probably haven't learned how to consciously create images. The simplest way to learn to make images at will is to practice.

SEEING SHAPES

Cut shapes out of construction paper and paste them onto white cardboard. The classic shapes are the circle, square, and triangle, but in this exercise you should also cut out a diamond shape. You can make them different colors; if you want to use the elemental colors, make a blue circle, green square, red triangle, and yellow diamond. However, you are free to use any shape or color you like.

Put one of the shapes in front of you. Sit comfortably. Use a breathing or energy exercise to ground and center. Look at the shape on the cardboard. Now close your eyes and see the shape. Open your eyes, look at the shape, and close your eyes again.

Work on each of the shapes for a few minutes. Do this exercise three times a week for three weeks.

At the end of three weeks of practicing this exercise, you will confidently be able to close your eyes and visualize any shape you like at will. You can further develop this skill by imagining objects.

SEEING OBJECTS

Locate a fairly complicated object, like a carnation
or an orange. Look at it. Close your eyes and visualize it. See the individual curves of the leaves, the
dimples on the orange, the subtle gradations of
color. Now turn it in your imagination, and look at
it from another angle.

If you can visualize an orange and turn it at will, you
have achieved excellent mastery of visualization skills.
Again, while some people find this easy, and some find it
difficult, every sighted person is able to visualize at conscious will.

Some magical operations require us to be able to close
our eyes and visualize for extended periods. It's easiest when
we're doing so to project the images onto a screen. This
screen floats about six inches in front of the forehead—if we
tilted our eyes up slightly, we'd be looking at it.

SEEING OBJECTS ON THE SCREEN

Close your eyes. Notice your image screen. See your
name clearly projected on the screen.

Magic and ritual often require visualizing shapes. We
trace energy in the air, and visualize it as we go. The following exercise requires being able to visualize with open
eyes. Again, some people find this commonplace, and
even easier to do than visualizing with eyes closed, while
others might find it more difficult. As with any visualization exercise, all it takes is practice.

SEEING WITH OPEN EYES

Close your eyes. Imagine an orange. Now open your
eyes and continue to see the orange, floating in front
of your eyes.

Physical background can make a difference when we're
visualizing with open eyes. A cluttered, busy background
can be distracting, breaking the concentration necessary
to make the image. This is why magicians often work in
spaces that are dedicated to magical work, usually called
temples. If the temple space has plain white walls it is
much easier to visualize with open eyes.

Another kind of open-eyed seeing involves seeing energy.
We might see the energy we use as we move around in the
temple. An easy way to begin seeing energy is to learn to see
the aura.

The aura is a field of energy that surrounds the body.
It's really an overlap of the energy body on the physical
body. The aura can lie right up against the skin or extend
quite some distance from the body, and it can be any
color at all. It's very easy to see, once we begin to look.

The following exercise can be done by yourself. It's a lot
of fun to work with a partner, and even more fun to work
with an entire group of people. You should start with the
Seeing Your Own Aura exercise, even if you go on to work
with a partner or a group.

SEEING YOUR OWN AURA

Turn the lights low. Stand looking into a mirror with
a blank wall behind you, preferably lightly colored.

Relax your eyes so that your focus is soft, and, keeping your eyes on the reflection, let your attention move to your peripheral vision. Write down what you see.

SEEING A PARTNER'S AURA

Have your partner stand in front of a blank, light-colored background in a softly lit room. Stand about four feet from your partner. Let your eyes fall into soft focus, and look at the edge of your partner's body shape with the edge of your vision. Write down what you see. Have your partner look at your aura and compare notes. How did you see your partner, and what did your partner see when looking in the mirror? How did your partner see you, and what did you see in the mirror? Was it the same or different?

GROUP AURA EXERCISE

Have one person stand in front of a blank, light-colored background in a softly lit room. Everyone else in the group looks at that person's aura and writes down what they see. Look at several people before you trade notes about what you see.

Often the first thing we notice when looking at someone's aura is a blue light floating close to the skin. This is something the eye sees naturally as we begin to look at an object with concentration. What we are looking for is a light that probably extends a foot or two from the body. Common colors include blue, green, yellow, and white.

We might find that we see spots or streaks of color. Parts of the body might be obscured by a black or red color. Physical ailments are reflected in the energy body, and looking at an aura, we might see spots or streaks near the damaged area of the body. Sometimes the aura will show an illness before any physical signs manifest.

In this chapter we learned to consciously visualize, to quiet the mind, and to see auras. In the next chapter we will work on the sense of hearing and learn to notice how we create internal sounds and use sounds in specifically magical ways.

four

Sound

Sound is the sense most of us are the least conscious of using. This is a harsh world for sounds. There are so many people living on the planet that it is very difficult to find a place in the world where humans are not making some sound, and in places, tremendous amounts of sound. Our machinery also increases sound volume, especially in the urban environment. Living next to a freeway makes us grateful for an afternoon in the country!

Below is an exercise that focuses just on sound. Various disciplines term exercises like this *be here now, uptime,* or *come to your senses.*

NOTICE THE WORLD: COUNT THE SOUNDS
Set a timer for one minute. Close your eyes. For one minute, count the sounds in your environment. How loud are they? What is their pitch? Can you identify what made those sounds?

This is an interesting exercise to do in many different environments: in a public place where lots of people are gathered, in a park or aviary where there are a lot of birds, or in the house. Identifying sounds can be particularly interesting. How many of us have played "What was that?" lying in our beds at night?

At one time I moved from a large city to a very small town in rural Washington. I started out playing my tape deck every day. I noticed that it was very quiet, and eventually learned to turn the music off and listen to the wind in the trees, the dogs barking across the valley, and the tiny creatures rustling in the grass. In the city I had grown up using music to mask the sounds of my environment; it was better to listen to a sound I chose than the sounds I could not escape. Living in an agricultural town, I learned to enjoy hearing, and to listen to music when I was truly able to pay attention to the sounds.

Now I live in a semideveloped county and work in the city. When I go to work I sometimes listen to music using an MP3 player. When I'm writing or Web surfing, I might play music as a soundtrack, but most often I open the window and listen to the birdsong in the neighboring forest.

Playlist

What music do you listen to? When do you listen to it? How does it make you feel? Do you play music as background noise without thinking about it?

In Western culture we are used to thinking of music as entertainment. In other cultures, music also serves magical purposes, such as to induce trance, to call spirits or drive them away, to set the pattern for a dance, or to make an offering to deities.

Another bias of Western culture is that there are those who make music and others who buy it. In folk cultures everyone joins in making the music. Making your own music, like making any other magical item, helps to bring home musical lessons, and generates music you need to do what you want it to do.

Drumming is one of the most basic forms of making music. Drumbeats generally fall in beats based on twos: **loud** soft **loud** soft. Double meters mimic the human body: we walk in a two-step (**one** two **one** two) and our hearts beat in double time (thump-**thump,** thump-**thump**). One thing you can do with a drum is to mimic a heartbeat. Humans find this irresistible; it's very easy to fall into trance while listening to a heartbeat.

DRUMBEAT

If you have a drum, you can use that. Otherwise, use two sticks, or clap your hands together. Set your timer for fifteen minutes. You might also tape record this session. Hit your drum or clap your hands in roughly a heartbeat meter; if you have a metronome, you can set it for 215 bpm. Keep going for the full fifteen minutes.

What did you think, see, and feel as you drummed for fifteen minutes? Was this difficult for you? Did you find yourself counting every minute, or were you surprised when the fifteen minutes was up? People often find it more interesting to hit a drum, which generates a low percussive beat and the vibration of a membrane, than to use hands or sticks, which generate a high sharp sound. Many people find drumming to be a pleasurable activity—so much so that world beat festivals are springing up all over the country, and drumming circles (where anyone with a drum can jump in and play along) are popular at summer fairs.

Some years ago my coven recorded a drumming session at 215 bpm that lasted for fifteen minutes. It involved both deep percussion, large drums (examples are dumbeks and djembis), and high percussion (like gourd rattles, claves, and eggs). Many cultures use the 215 bpm meter to induce trance. We fell into trance while we were making that tape, and now we use it whenever we do trance work in coven. Listening to the tape automatically puts us in a suggestive state. This is one of the possible uses of the tape you made.

Some cultures use percussion to clear out the energy in a physical space. Tibetan Buddhist orchestras use large hand-held cymbals and long, raucous horns to chase away negative energies in a space.

Get Thee Gone!

Choose a time for this exercise when you will not
be disturbing your neighbors or roommates. Pick

up a pan and a spoon or a party noisemaker—anything that will make a lot of racket. Walk around your space banging on the pan or blowing in the noisemaker.

You can choose to say or shout something as you go, like "This space is clean!" Do you notice any difference in your house after the noisemaking? How do you feel about being in your space? One good time to do this is when you've had a fight and a lot of negative energy is hanging around the house.

Magical operations often use percussion to mark a particular place in the ceremony. We might clap hands at the end of a rite to dispel any lingering energies, or we can use sharp percussion at the beginning of a ritual to clear the space for the energies we will invoke. We might also strike a melodic bell to mark a place in the ritual where the energy shifts.

Most often, magicians use the voice in magical operations. This is a tremendously flexible instrument. It can do almost anything we need to do to make a sound happen. Magicians speak magical words, phrases and incantations, and names of power. We can vary the voice, speaking some words in a higher pitch, and names of power in a lower pitch.

One thing magicians learn to do early on is to read magical phrases in a firm, solemn voice called *intoning.*

Read a Poem

Find a place to work where you can be by yourself and not be overheard by anyone else: your apartment, your room, the bathroom, in the middle of a field in a public park, wherever you can find some personal space. Pick a poem that you enjoy. Read it out loud to yourself. Read one line very fast, and the next line very slowly. Read the next line loudly, and the one after that softly. Speak one line in a very high voice, and one in a very low voice. Now combine these: read a line in a high, soft, fast voice, and read another line in a low, loud, slow voice.

It is more important to know the range of your voice and to be able to vary how you are saying what you are saying than it is to produce any particular affect.

The specific technique magicians use when working with words of power is to *vibrate* them. To learn to vibrate a sound, we must learn our own *vibrational note*. The vibrational note is a particular frequency to which our body resonates. We can easily find our note by vocalizing a vowel.

Find Your Vibrational Note

In a private place, take a deep breath, open your mouth fairly widely, and sound the vowel sound "ah" on a single note. Start with a fairly low note. Take another breath and sound "ah" on a somewhat higher note. Keep going up in pitch, and then back down. One of the notes that you sound will have a different feeling: you might feel a jolt, or a tingling, or a resonance in your chest. You might hear a different sound, as if it is bigger, or thicker. That note is your particular vibrational note.

The thicker sounds you hear are overtones, or harmonics. Each note you say or sing has overtones, but when you hit the vibrational note, you can hear them more clearly. Some singing traditions, like the religious tradition of Tibetan Buddhist monks, emphasize the harmonic sounds to the extent that it seems there is more than one voice making the sound coming out of a single throat. You can add the power of overtones to voice.

SINGING THE OVERTONES

Stand facing a wall so that the sound you make will bounce back to you easily. You can also try this exercise in the shower. Sound your vibrational note by shaping your mouth into an "oh." Arch the roof of your mouth while opening the back of your throat. If the idea is still a little vague, just arch the roof of your mouth. Listen for the higher sounds in addition to the note that you are singing.

If you keep practicing this exercise, you will find it easier and easier to hear the overtones. You don't have to be a good singer to be able to use the magical voice or to hear and use overtones. You're not trying to match a particular pitch, or to move from one pitch to another. You're just finding the place where you yourself vibrate while making that sound. The note can vary in pitch. The important thing is making the sound that feels right magically.

Many cultures use the voice to induce a trance state in the singer and in the listener. A chant is a fairly short song with just a few words or a vowel sung to just a few repeated notes. The simplest form of chant is to sing vowels to a single note.

Chant the Vowels

Set a timer for one minute. Sing "ah ay ee i oh ooh" on a single note, preferably your vibrational note. Arch the roof of your mouth to accentuate the overtones.

What did you think about, see, hear, or feel during the minute that you were chanting? Many people find the repetition of sounds to be very hypnotic, soothing, and quieting. This is another practice you can do to quiet the mind before ritual.

In group work it can be very helpful for all to chant "om" or to do the vowel chant before working magic. The chanting brings everyone's disparate energies into harmony with each other and provides a group centering that can then be focused on the specific magic at hand.

These are all ways that we can make sounds externally. What about the sounds that we make internally? Most of us have internalized voices that tell us things about ourselves. Sometimes they come from our parents, or teachers, or later in life our lovers and spouses. Sometimes they tell us positive things; at other times they reinforce negative beliefs, occasionally to the extent that we become paralyzed and unable to do certain things or believe in ourselves. Many forms of therapy deal with identifying voices saying negative things and learning to face them and override them.

Turn the Sound Off

If you become aware of a voice telling you negative things about yourself, imagine that you are turning down the volume of it using a volume dial. The voice gets quieter and quieter until finally you turn the sound completely off.

We can also use this technique to deal with music that gets stuck in our head. Another way we can gain control of a song-gone-amuck is by choosing to listen to another song—the DJ inside our head substitutes our own tune for the one we are haplessly repeating. If we use the same song as the substitute song each time we get stuck on the music, we can combine these two techniques. Just switch the stuck music to the overwrite song, then use the volume control to turn it down and then off.

Similarly, we can overwrite the negative voices in our heads with positive voices by giving ourselves *affirmations*. Affirmations are statements that we say to ourselves about things we wish to manifest. They are sentences that we can say out loud or silently to ourselves using the internal sense of hearing.

Here are a couple of good rules of thumb for writing affirmations:

1. **Use the present tense.** Say "I am," not "I am becoming" or "I will be." If we put the affirmation in the future, it never arrives! Make the affirmation in the present, and it has already happened.

2. **Use the positive, drop the negative.** Say "I am beautiful," not "I am not ugly." This is a difficult but very important rule to use. If we say "I am not ugly," we are making an image and starting from an assumption that we are ugly. We manifest the ugly first and then try to counteract that, which is very hard to do. When we say "I am beautiful," all that energy is going into making the beauty happen.

3. **Specify what, not how.** Say, "I have a job that is perfect for me," instead of "I get the job I applied for this week." If we specify what, we limit ourselves. The job you applied for this week might turn out to be low paying, while a job you apply for next week turns out to pay much better with great benefits.

Now we are ready to make our own affirmations.

MAKE AN AFFIRMATION

Create an affirmation that helps you to complete your exercises. Are you having trouble finding time to do them, or concentrating on them, or believing

you can do them? Is there one exercise that is especially hard to do? Make an affirmation that helps
you get through this. Examples:

- I have plenty of time to do my exercises.

- I concentrate easily on my exercises.

- I easily complete my exercises.

- I make my vibrational tone strong and clear.

Write the affirmation on a card. Say it out loud
to yourself. Put the card in a place where only you
can see it, such as your bedroom door or the inside
cover of a notebook.

In this chapter we learned to pay conscious attention to
sounds, vary the voice and make the vibrational note, and
make affirmations to manifest results. Next we will work
on feeling the world, noticing internal sensations, and
moving energy by moving our bodies in physical space.

five

Feeling and Movement

Skill in feeling moving energy is critical to successful magic. While sight and sound are senses that we associate with specific organs of the body (the eyes and ears), feeling is a sense that we experience with the entire body. We feel the world sensitively with the surface of the skin. In fact, our skin registers the shock and frequency of sounds, so the entire body participates in hearing. As we register light and warmth on our skin, the body also participates in seeing. And as energy moves within us and surrounds us, we also move energy when we move in physical space. The sense of feeling is the most complicated of all the senses.

Notice the World: Feel the Air

Practice this exercise in a comfortable environment, preferably indoors and in private, at least the first time. Wear as little clothing as you can; if you

are comfortable with nudity, or you want to experiment with the sensation, take all your clothes off.
Walk around the room. Notice the air on your skin.
What temperature is it? If there is a breeze in the
room, how does it feel? If you like, you can set up a
fan and stand in front of it. Does the air feel the
same all over your body, or different in different
places? Can you feel the air more sensitively with
some parts of your body than with others?

Nudists are people who enjoy the sensation of air against
their skin. If you wish to explore the feel of air against your
skin outdoors, you can contact a nudist colony in your
area. I have visited a number of these, and they are always
quite friendly, family oriented, and happy to give you a
tour. You can bring a friend along if you feel shy about
going alone!

We all learned to walk when we were very, very young,
and as we grow older the movements involved with walking become totally outside our conscious awareness. Paying attention to the process of walking is a good beginning step in paying attention to where our bodies are in
space and the energy we push along when we move.

CONSCIOUS WALKING

Do this exercise in a comfortable space. You can do
it with or without your clothes on. Set a timer for
one minute. Stand with your feet about a shoulder's width apart, arms at your sides. Bend your
knees slightly. Focus your attention on your one

point. Now slowly step forward with one leg, putting your heel down first, and then rolling onto the ball of your foot. Shifting smoothly, step forward with your other foot, again putting your heel down first and then rolling onto the ball of your foot. Continue to walk slowly, rolling onto and off from both feet. When you need to turn, notice how your hips rotate, and move slowly into the curve of the turn.

This is a good exercise to do in conjunction with energy exercises like the Tree or the Mountain. We can also try adding a breathing exercise: exhale as a foot comes down, inhale as the foot lifts up. Conscious movement is the foundation of bodywork disciplines and martial arts. When you do this exercise, be aware of the energy in your body. What is its temperature and color? Where is it moving? Where is it blocked?

When we ask each other "How do you feel?" we are generally not talking about sensing air temperature. The question asks us to talk about our internal state, our sense of being in the world, and in particular, what emotions we might be experiencing.

Emotions are easy to name but difficult to define. Cognitive researchers recognize six basic human emotions called *affects* in every human being anywhere on the planet from birth onward. Affects are expressed through facial expressions, which are universal to humans. The six emotions are happiness, anger, grief, fear, shame, and disgust.

EXPRESSING EMOTION

Stand in front of a mirror. Make a face that expresses anger. Now make a face that expresses fear. Work your way through the emotions: grief, shame, disgust. End with the expression that expresses happiness.

Anger is a frown; grief pulls the face down. Disgust is the face a baby makes while spitting out food, and fear widens the eyes. Shame is a flaming, ducked head wanting to hide, and happiness is a smile. One thing you might notice is that as you make the face, you find yourself feeling the emotion. The facial expression is a trigger—we are used to feeling the emotion when we are making that face. As our emotions grow more complicated, we associate many triggers with them.

Emotions are also expressed in internal sensations. Some of them are physically based. For example, fear might release adrenaline, which causes the body to shake. Some of them are also learned. Many people share similar feelings, but there are sensations that are unique to each of us that we have learned to identify with particular emotions. Noticing the physical sensations can help identify the feelings associated with them.

SENSING EMOTION

Make a list: What do you feel inside your body when you feel happy? Sad? Angry? Afraid? Are there muscles that clench? Do you have a trembling in a particular body part? Do you feel hot or cold?

You might feel hot when you are angry, or get a knot in your stomach. I have a sensation of dizziness and a trembling in my solar plexus when I am angry. You will find that as you pay conscious attention to what you feel, you will become more sensitive to emotional nuances.

Knowing what we are feeling is the first step toward the magical discipline of emotion. The magician exercises emotional control in daily life, choosing when to express emotion and when to refrain from doing so. We may not have a choice about what emotion we experience to a given trigger, but we do have the choice about how we will act it out. When we find ourselves overwhelmed with emotion, we can ground it out in the same way that we ground out energy.

GROUNDING EMOTION

Close your eyes. Visualize yourself filled with and surrounded by energy. It has the color and temperature and texture of the emotion you are feeling: hot, red anger; cold, blue fear. Now take a deep breath and exhale, visualizing and feeling the energy flowing down into the earth. As you breathe in, see warm golden light filling you and surrounding you.

This is one of the most difficult exercises to do. It helps to remember that the emotion and the person feeling the emotion are different. The same person can feel many emotions. When one overwhelms us, we can find that sense of calm and strength within us, and move out of that emotional state into peace.

In addition to controlling emotions that we experience in our day-to-day life, the magician will often be called upon to generate a specific emotion in a ritual. Most often that emotion is enthusiasm or passion.

Generating Enthusiasm

Find a poem or story that generates a feeling of enthusiasm in you—for example, Walt Whitman's *Song of Myself*. When you are alone and you know you won't be disturbed, read it out loud to yourself. Be as flamboyant and exaggerated as you can bring yourself to be while reading the piece.

Acting as if you feel passion can trigger the feeling of enthusiasm and excitement. Even if the feeling isn't immediately there, if you continue the reading and put yourself into the piece, the enthusiasm you bring to the performance will generate the energy you need. This works in performing ritual—even if we don't immediately feel passionate, we can generate passion by reading the ritual words forcefully and confidently.

We express passion with the voice by infusing it with intensity. We also express passion with movement by making large, decisive gestures. Magical gesturing is a very quick and effective way to generate and move energy. In general, movements of the arms and legs toward the body generate closed and protected circular energy, while movements of the arms and legs away from the body direct energy outward.

The most economical gestures are those made by the hands. By placing the hand in a particular position, we can evoke a deity, move energy within the body, and throw energy out into the world with specific intent. We can associate particular hand gestures with particular states of mind. Whenever we make the gesture, we trigger the state we intend to induce.

The Meditation Gesture

Sit cross-legged, or kneel back on your heels. Set a timer for one minute. Place your hands on your knees, palms down. Inhale, and turn your hands upward, bringing your thumb to your index finger. For one minute do a breathing meditation. When the timer rings, place your hands back on your knees, palms down.

Repeating this exercise deepens the trigger association. Soon you will find yourself falling into a meditative trance the moment your hands turn over and make a circle with your finger and thumb.

A gesture magical people sometimes make in ordinary conversation is a protective gesture. When someone says something negative like, "I hope I don't get in an accident today," make a horn of the hand by dropping your two middle fingers and placing the thumb on them, leaving your index and pinky fingers extended. With your fingers pointing straight ahead, draw the horn smartly across your chest. This gesture means "Let this pass without happening." You can visualize your hand pushing the energy of the idea away to let it dissipate harmlessly.

Another protective gesture is to tuck the thumb inside a fist. This has the effect of closing off the energy of the body, as if we are shielding ourselves. This is a good gesture to use when we are in a place where we do not feel comfortable.

Most magical gestures involve moving the entire body. There are specific postures magicians adopt in doing ritual magic. We normally do two of them quite a bit: sitting and standing!

SIT ON A CHAIR

Sit on a chair with your knees spread slightly, arms lying along your upper legs. Hold your back straight and your head erect, just as if you are royalty sitting on a throne.

This is an excellent posture for scrying, or doing concentration exercises. The cross-legged position described above is one of the yogic asanas; those who find this easy might be interested in exploring variations on that movement. The act of sitting back on the heels comes from the aikido tradition.

SIT ON YOUR HEELS

Kneel on the floor, keeping your body erect. Place one of your big toes on the other and spread your knees slightly. Now lower your buttocks onto your heels.

This is a surprisingly comfortable position to maintain for long periods of time. People who find it difficult to sit cross-legged sometimes find this position easier to maintain. It has the added advantage of bringing all the chakras into alignment. We'll talk more about chakras in chapter 7.

LIE DOWN

Lie on the floor, keeping your body straight and your arms at your sides.

This is a posture we might find ourselves using if we are doing a very deep meditation, or if we are attempting astral projection or another operation that might cause the body to fall over. However, it is easy to fall asleep in this position! If you find yourself growing sleepy, you can shift to a sitting position.

These three positions—sitting, standing, and lying—are the ones we will use in rituals when we are being still. However, magicians also move around. The simplest movement is to walk around in a circle.

CIRCUMAMBULATION

Find a space where you can walk in a fairly large circle. Start in the eastern section of the room and face the wall. Slowly turn to your right (toward the south) and, walking consciously, slowly move in a circle around the room. When you have reached the place where you started, slowly turn and face the wall again.

> Now turn and circle the room again. This time
> add a vowel chant, sounding the vowel "ah" with
> your vibrational voice as you move. End the chant
> when you turn back toward the wall.

Every ritual that creates a ritual space will include some variation on this simple circumambulation. Magicians generate energy vortexes by moving the entire body around in space. The energy vortex can be designed to create a circular or spherical space in which the magician works. It can invoke a particular kind of energy or it can set up a whirlwind that will be sent out for a particular purpose.

Circumambulations, and most magical movements, will usually start and end in the east to align with the energy of the sunrise, a powerful metaphor for spiritual enlightenment. Circumambulations usually go clockwise from east to south to west to north, but there are exceptions to this. Magicians who work in the Southern Hemisphere sometimes prefer to work counterclockwise, as that is the direction of the earth's energy field. Sometimes magicians refer to the clockwise motion as *deosil,* and the counterclockwise motion as *widdershins.*

Interestingly, most folk dances, especially line dances, go widdershins. Folk dancers talk about *line of direction,* which is the way the line of dancers is facing. The dances often start on the right leg, which is usually dominant, so the dancers move counterclockwise.

Dance is sometimes used in a circular direction to create ritual space, but much more often it is used to generate a particular kind of energy or to induce trance. The world's cultures are filled with body movements that hypnotically rock the brain to sleep. The following is a very popular one, rediscovered by children the world over.

ROCKING TRANCE

Sit on a chair or on the floor cross-legged or on your heels; choose a posture in which you can rock comfortably. Set a timer for one minute. Rock your torso forward as far as you can, and then back, and then forward again. Rock at a pace you find comfortable. Make a sound if you are inspired to do so.

This is a good exercise to combine with a simple one-vowel chant. The rocking trance belongs in the arsenal of trance inductions.

SPINNING TRANCE

Do this exercise in a space clear of furniture. Set your timer for one minute, and spin slowly. If you find yourself becoming dizzy, stop and spin in the other direction.

It's a handy trick to know that if you become dizzy, spinning once in the other direction will help you gain your bearings again. Sufi mystics (called *whirling dervishes* by some) use the spinning trance as a form of spiritual meditation.

Magicians use specific gestures to move energy. The two that are used most often are piercing and the pentagram.

Piercing

Stand with your feet a shoulder's width apart. Lift your arms, bending them at the elbows, and bring your hands close to your head a shoulder's width apart. Now step forward smartly on your dominant foot, while at the same time pushing your arms forward so that they are both pointing in the direction you have stepped.

Pentagram

Stand with your feet a shoulder's width apart. Lift your dominant arm and hold it in front of your left knee. Now bring it up in a line toward a point just in front of the middle of your forehead. Drop it back down again to your right knee. Move it upward again toward your left shoulder. The next movement is a horizontal cross over to your right shoulder. Finally, drop your hand back down toward your left knee. (See Figure 1.)

You can combine the two gestures by piercing the center of the pentagram after you have drawn it. The pentagram in the exercise is a banishing earth pentagram. Golden Dawn magicians will use it to banish the element of earth, or heaviness, in a space. Witches use it to banish negative energies in a space.

In this section we have learned to move consciously, observe our emotions, and move energy with gestures and movements. Next we will combine all of the senses, learning to live in the world with a quiet mind using our

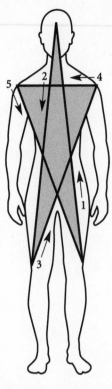

Figure 1. The Pentagram exercise.

senses, and we will practice a manifestation technique. We will also learn to expand our senses, using simple psychic development exercises to sense the future and send and receive thoughts.

Using All the Senses

It is important in magical training to separate the senses and learn to control each individually. However, our normal experience of life involves using all the senses simultaneously. Although we have learned to view them as discrete, in practice the senses tend to blend into one another. Some phenomenologists believe that our physical senses—sight, sound, hearing, taste, and smell—are ways that the mind splits out our primal experience of the world. They believe that all these senses are rooted in a sense far below the threshold of consciousness, a single mode of perception sometimes called the *common sense.* Some psychics take this a step further, believing that this common sense also collects information that does not easily fall into any of the normal categories of sight, sound, and feeling, such as images about the future, what people are thinking, and the state of the energy environment around us.

Be Here Now

As with the individual sense exercises, we begin our exploration of the common sense by placing our attention entirely with the physical senses.

NOTICE THE WORLD

Set your timer for one minute. Observe the world around you. Look at the colors and shapes and the people around you. Listen to the sounds surrounding you. Feel the temperature of the air, the pressure of the chair you are sitting on, or the floor beneath your feet.

It can be a profound experience to move through the world paying attention to just the input of the physical senses. Some people experience a kind of rapture through living entirely in the physical world. It is the most profound kind of grounding—the grounding of being in this body, in this place, at this time. Most of us spend a great deal of time thinking about what we have done and what we are going to do. Philosophers remind us that the present moment is all that actually exists. This is an exercise that becomes a way of life.

Memory

When we think about the past, we inhabit memories that capture the moment that formed them. We experience the sights, sounds, and feelings we experienced in the past. Most of us are primarily aware of one of those senses—

usually feeling, sometimes seeing, rarely hearing. Now that we have practiced visualizing, making sounds, and paying attention to our feelings, we should be able to approach memory with the recognition of all the senses involved.

Memory is slippery. Some memories have to be rehearsed to be maintained, and others will come back with crystal clarity if something triggers them, like a particular scent. In addition to sight, sound, and feeling, memories encode information from our other senses, including smell and taste. Scent is a powerful memory trigger; get a whiff of freshly mown grass or blackboard chalk and we are suddenly catapulted back to childhood and the experience we had running across a lawn or standing in front of a class.

These next exercises practice retrieving memories and explore the nature of remembrance.

Yesterday

Think about what you did yesterday in backward order—from the moment you went to bed to the moment you got up. Pick a day in the last week and remember that one in the same way. Try to remember a day in the last month.

Baby Thoughts

What's your oldest memory? Write it down. Is this a memory that you have kept private, or one that you discussed with your family? What is your oldest memory that you have never told anyone?

BIRTHDAYS

What did you do on your most recent birthday?
What was your favorite birthday? What is your earliest birthday memory?

As with many exercises in this book, it's helpful to
return to the Yesterday exercise occasionally as we continue to develop magical skill. In ritual magic we often
enter deep trance states. As we return to normal consciousness, it can be very difficult to recall what happened
during the trance state. Sharpening recollection skill by
recalling what we did yesterday helps us learn to recover
memories made under many different circumstances.

Dreamwork

Another practice that helps develop the memory is dreamwork. We all dream every night. If we didn't, we'd lose our
mental balance! The trick is to remember what we have
dreamed. That is a learned skill that usually takes some
practice to pick up.

REMEMBER DREAMS

Before you go to sleep, give yourself the firm affirmation, "I remember my dreams." Keep a pen and
paper beside your bed. Sometimes we wake up a little bit at the end of each dream cycle. If you come
awake enough to remember the pen and paper, jot
down a few key words describing the images of

your dreams. Otherwise, do this when you wake up
in the morning.

Many people say "I don't dream." What they really
mean is that they don't remember their dreams. Physical
processes can make remembering dreams difficult. Some
drugs also tend to drive dreams so deep that it's hard to
bring them to consciousness. However, if we persist in
this exercise, we will be able to remember more of our
dreams.

During the day, as close to waking up as possible, look
at the key words in your dream notes. They should jog
your memory and permit you to recover more of the
dream. "Roller coaster, baby, sister," lets you bring back
the dream sequence, "I was riding on a roller coaster,
holding a baby. When the roller coaster stopped, the baby
turned into my sister." Another key point about recording
dreams is to try to remember what happened without
suppressing or changing the image. Since people don't
turn into other people in real life, you might be tempted
to say, "I gave the baby to my sister," and alter the meaning
of the dream. The key is to respect the dream image and
try to recover it exactly as it happened.

Dreams have their own conventions that take some
getting used to. Things can happen simultaneously or on
multiple levels that would not happen during waking life,
and that are different from the conventions of Hollywood
movies. Examples of dream processes include a voice
explaining what is happening, people shapeshifting into

other people, and the point of view shifting from one dream character to another, or inhabiting two or more dream characters at once.

Recording our dreams over time gives us an invaluable key to understanding the issues that are important to us. We can examine the dream record for images that recur. We might notice that we frequently dream about babies, or roller coasters, or our high school French teacher, and gradually become clear on what that image means to us. I recommend avoiding dream symbolism books with canned meanings such as "Seeing a carrot means that you will be receiving money," because dream images are so individual. While it is true that our culture tends to weight certain images with meaning (i.e., red means anger or passion), we each have our own unique take on it.

As we grow more proficient in remembering dreams, we can begin to work with the imagery. One helpful thing to do is to complete the dream during the day. The dream has put processes into motion, and very frequently those processes don't get completed. We can complete them while awake, moving the processes into another phase, and opening out new insights into your own dream imagery.

COMPLETING THE DREAM

In the dream you started an action that you did not finish. For example, you set out to go to your brother's house, but got sidetracked and ended up at a grocery store. When you wake up, visualize yourself at the last point in your dream, such as in

the parking lot of the grocery store. See and feel
yourself going to your brother's house and knock-
ing on the door.

It can be frustrating or confusing to abandon a project
in the middle of a dream. Finishing it can free up knotted
emotions, bringing a sense of calm and accomplishment.

We can also learn more about our dreams by talking to
the characters in our dreams.

Talking to the Dream

For example, in the dream, your sister jumped out
of the roller coaster and said, "I'm going home to
do my hair!" That was confusing to you. When you
wake up, sit quietly and imagine yourself back in
the roller coaster looking at your sister. Say, "Why
did you say you were going home to do your hair?"
Listen to her response. For example, she could say,
"Because I am spending too much time having fun
and not enough time taking care of myself."

Psychic Development

One of the things I did as a beginning magical practi-
tioner was to develop my psychic senses. These development techniques rest on the physical and inner-sense
exercises we have already been doing.

The first thing we do is to reach out to sense the world
around us.

What's Around the Corner?

Try this exercise the next time you are in a grocery store. Look all the way down to the end of the aisle. Now push beyond it, around the corner. Can you sense what is around the corner? Is a person heading in your direction, or is there a shelf system or display there?

Master martial artists sometimes demonstrate the ability to move energy by asking a subject to close his or her eyes, and then tapping on the subject's knee using energy alone. This exercise is based on that kind of energy projection. This can be very useful when you need to see around you—say, at night when you're lying in bed trying to identify that sound!

Seeing the World

Try this exercise while you are lying in bed. Imagine yourself growing until you are the size of your house. You look around and see all the spaces around your house, all the houses in the neighborhood, and the cars on the street.

We can use the psychic sense to discover who is trying to communicate with us.

Who's on the Phone?

The next time the phone rings, stop for a second to clear your mind. Ask yourself the question, "Who's on the phone?" Immediately verbalize the first thing

that comes to your mind—for example, "Harry."
Then pick up the phone and see who it is.

In this kind of sensing work, the most important thing is to report whatever you are seeing and feeling without editing. We are very accustomed to editing out the information we get from our psychic senses. The conscious mind rationalizes it away: "It can't be Harry. How could I possibly know that? I want it to be Harry, and that's why I think it is." If it is Harry, we say to ourselves, "That's a coincidence."

In training psychic skills, we emphasize reporting whatever it is we see and hear without editing. Just notice, record, and report whatever the image or sound or feeling is.

We use extended senses to explore the future, or worlds beyond this one. The term most often used to describe this is *scrying*. We can scry by projecting images into an object like a bowl of water or a crystal ball, or we can close our eyes and see the image on our visualization screen.

Scrying

Do this exercise in a space where you can be alone. Fill a dark bowl with water. Sit in front of it. Do a centering exercise, like sending roots into the ground, and use one of your trance inductions, like sounding a single vowel. The idea is to clear your mind. Now say to yourself, "I see what will happen tomorrow," and look in the bowl. Notice any images that float in your mind when you do this, any sounds you hear, any sensations in your body.

Close your eyes, bring up your visualization screen,
and notice any images that appear there. Record
your results.

In the beginning you might think you don't see anything, or you might see something that makes no sense to
you at the time. Just record whatever impressions you get:
"I saw a gray cloud, and I felt cold." Follow up on this
exercise. Before you go to bed, sit down and remember all
the things you did during the day. Perhaps you entered a
gray, air-conditioned hall.

We can use this exercise to see other people. To do this,
it's helpful to team up with a friend who is willing to
work with you. Conduct the experiment at a prearranged
time. Tell your friend to write down his or her impressions of the place he or she is in at the exact moment of
the experiment. At the same time ask the scrying question, "What is my friend doing right now?" Later you can
compare notes about what your friend experienced and
what you experienced.

You need a partner to conduct telepathy exercises.

TELEPATHY

Choose a time when both of you can spend a few
minutes concentrating. Choose one person to be
the sender, and one person to be the receiver. The
sender picks out an object, like a blue ball, and concentrates on it. The receiver sits quietly, clears the
mind, and permits the image to form on his or her
visualization screen.

After you've been practicing this exercise for a while, you might find that you hear strong thoughts from the people around you. Someone thinks, "It's a hot day today," and you respond, "It sure is hot isn't it!" Sometimes people become aware of this and say, "Boy, I didn't think I said that out loud."

This can be a helpful skill to have if you need to urgently contact someone you can't reach in any other way. Sit, clear your mind, visualize the person, and say very clearly, "Call me. It's very important!" The other person may not receive a clear image or sound, but may be inexplicably moved to call you. Or, he or she may report hearing your voice very clearly.

We can also communicate with people while they are asleep. The image or words that we project show up in their dreams. We can also explore expanding our senses in our own dreams.

DREAMING TOMORROW

Before you go to sleep, give yourself the affirmation, "I dream about the future day before me." When you wake up, record your dreams.

The dreams that we have about the future can seem very real; it becomes difficult to tell the dream from a memory. That's another reason it is important to write down both our dreams and our magical workings. I once dreamed that a friend of mine went out on a date with a new girlfriend. When I saw him the next day, I said automatically, "How did your date go?" He did a double take and said, "I didn't tell you about that date!" At that second I realized I had seen him in a dream. I said, "Oh, of course you did!" and he accepted the rationalization and told me how much fun he had had.

One caution about precognition exercises: we almost never get exact information. One very common thing beginners do is to try to see the numbers of the winning lottery tickets. This is a very difficult procedure to pull off; the numbers are so randomly chosen, and so many people are competing to see them, that it's almost impossible to get this right. We can certainly try, and we might succeed, but our time and energy are probably better spent on other manifestation techniques.

Innerspace

The most helpful technique I use to manifest the results I want combines all the skills based on the senses. *Innerspace* uses visualizations, affirmations, and future-pacing (see chapter 13 for more about future-pacing) to bring about what we wish to pass.

Innerspace is a form of trance induction that has been called *self-hypnosis*. It induces a state in which the mind is suggestible, and in which we can generate the energy needed to make changes in the plastic world of possibility. The trance induction uses four key words. Each of these words is linked to a state: physical relaxation, emotional calm, mental clarity, and trance.

Choosing your relaxation word. Think of a time you were physically relaxed—for example, in a warm bath, just before falling asleep, or after a physical workout. If you have never felt this, imagine what it would be like. Pick a short word that captures this feeling for you and write it down. If you can't think of any word, you can use the word *relax*.

Choosing your calm word. Think of a time you were at peace; when you had a sense of warm belonging, that all was right with the world. Some examples are the middle of summer as a child, in your room surrounded by your own stuff, and just after a good meal. If you have never felt this, imagine what it would be like. Pick a short word that captures this feeling for you and write it down. If you can't think of any word, you can use the word *calm*.

Choosing your mental clarity word. Think of a time you were mentally sharp and felt in control of your thoughts—for example, while you were taking an easy test, or reading a book you suddenly understood. If you have never felt this, imagine what it would be like. Pick a short word that captures this feeling for you and write it down. If you can't think of any word, you can use the word *focus*.

Choosing your trance word. Think of a time you felt as if anything was possible. For example, when you graduated from high school and had your whole adult life in front of you, when you woke up in the morning and realized you had the whole summer ahead of you, when you won an award, or passed a difficult test. If you have never felt this, imagine what it would be like. Pick a short word that captures this feeling for you and write it down. If you can't think of any word, you can use the word *power.*

Choosing your return word. Think of a time you moved from one state of awareness to another—for example, waking up in the morning, ending a good novel and putting it down, or noticing the room. If you have never felt this, imagine what it would be like. Pick a short word that captures this feeling for you and write it down. If you can't think of any word, you can use the word *return.*

Write these words down. Memorize them if you can.

Entering Innerspace

Do this exercise in a private place. Do a centering exercise. Take a deep breath and exhale completely. Close your eyes. Bring up your visualization screen, which is just in front of your eyes and a little bit above them. See your relaxation word on the screen and say it out loud. Next, see and say your calm word. See and say your focus word. See and say your trance word. Say to yourself, "I am now in my innerspace, a space I can enter at any time, for any purpose I desire." Notice any feelings or images you have at that moment.

Now see and say to yourself your relaxation word, your calm word, your focus word, and your return word. Open your eyes. Get up, stretch, and walk around.

If you find this difficult to do at first, you can tape record yourself saying slowly, "See and say to yourself the word *relax.*" Then play the tape while you do the exercise. People often report feeling their bodies getting warm and relaxed while doing this exercise.

The innerspace is your key to manifestation. In this space you can create any experience for yourself that you want. There are two immediate things to do here: build your personal relaxation space and give yourself affirmations.

Our personal relaxation space is a place we can go to any time we like, a place where we are safe, warm, and relaxed. Think of a natural place where you would like to have a vacation home. Do you enjoy the mountains? Build yourself a log cabin. Do you like the desert? Your relaxation space is an adobe house with weavings on the walls. Is the ocean your summertime destination? You can have a house on a cliff overlooking the waves.

BUILDING YOUR RELAXATION SPACE

Go into innerspace by saying your relaxation, calm, focus, and trance words. Say to yourself, "I am in my relaxation space." Look around. What is the room you are in? How big is it? Does it have furniture? You can put a window in a wall and look outside. What is the temperature? The adobe house might be cool compared to the hot desert sun, and the log cabin is warm compared to the cool mountain air.

Now bring yourself back out of innerspace by saying your relaxation, calm, focus, and return words.

The relaxation space is an internal vacation home that you can decorate any way you like. When I enter my innerspace, I am sitting on a window seat overlooking the ocean. The window seat is in a kitchen, which is warmly decorated with light-colored woods and yellow curtains. In this kitchen I keep many remedies that help me in my life: sleep potions, drinks to settle my stomach, and just drinks that warm me up when I'm cold.

We can also do any of the psychic development exercises in our relaxation space. My house has a room containing an enormous movie screen. I can say to the screen, "Show me what my friend is doing this moment." I don't use it for telepathy experiments often though; what I use it for most is to project energy into the future.

My Day Tomorrow

Go to your innerspace. Bring up your visualization screen or view a screen that is in your relaxation space. Now see yourself going through your day tomorrow. As you watch this movie, give yourself affirmations about the day. For example, "I am relaxed and confident during the meeting. My presentation goes off very well, and I receive many compliments on it," or "I get the test back and see that I have passed with flying colors." Feel how happy you are as you realize that you have passed the test.

Remember the affirmation guidelines: use the present tense, use positive words, and specify what, not how.

In this chapter we have learned memory exercises, dreamwork, and innerspace manifestation. Next we will work with the energy of the body again, learning to shield and to energize and clear chakras.

Working with Energy Fields

We are accustomed to thinking of the world as being composed of either energy or matter. That's a true and valid point of view and it is helpful for doing certain kinds of science. Another valid way of looking at the world is that everything in it is a form of energy. There are differences in the types of energy; each individual energy interacts in different ways with its neighbors. Ritual magicians learn how to sense, observe, and work with those energies.

We'll start with our own energy field. We've practiced moving the aura, and observing our own and other people's auras. The auras of untrained people tend to flow into the energies of the places surrounding it. Magicians learn how to harden the edge of the aura, so that we consciously choose when we will exchange energy, permitting some energies to interact with us while excluding those that are harmful to our physical and emotional health.

Hardening the aura generates what some magical disciplines call a *shield*. A shield is an energy wall that we can choose to put into place and take down at any time.

THE SHIELD

Do this exercise in a place where you will not be disturbed. First, center yourself. Visualize and sense your aura as it is now. Now visualize and feel your aura forming an oval or egg shape about a foot from your physical skin. Visualize and feel a layer of white light coating the outside of this shield, starting above your head and moving down around the surface of the shield until it reaches the space between your feet. Give yourself an affirmation: "My aura is impermeable when I wish it to be," or "I raise my shield whenever I desire." Take a deep breath, let it out, and relax your aura, allowing it to return to its starting color/temperature/location.

Continue to practice this exercise until you can snap your shield into place the second you think about it. Experiment with different colors; try making the shield out of red, blue, green, or yellow light. Do you experience different temperatures, textures, or hardnesses with different colors?

We can use the shield to protect ourselves when we are in the presence of someone whose energy we wish to avoid. For example, if someone is shouting at us and throwing anger in our direction, we can shield ourselves and choose to separate ourselves from the anger energy. This can also help us to avoid becoming angry ourselves.

We have worked with the energy channels in the body: the central column, and also the channels flowing down the arms and legs. When we generate energy fields and channel energy to charge an object, we will direct energy along the central column. It is important that energy flows freely through the central column. To check on that, we will take a look at the centers of energy located along the central column: the chakras (see Figure 2).

Chakra means "wheel," and that's just what they are: wheels or circulating spheres of energy. They act like the organs of the energy body, concentrating and directing particular kinds of energy. Different traditions recognize different chakras, although there is a great deal of overlap between them. You may find that you recognize energy centers at other places than those listed here. However, you will almost certainly find that you have at least the following chakras.

The crown chakra. This sphere, usually visualized as white, is located a little above your head. This chakra gives out and takes in energy, and collects and directs energies we might call spiritual. In those people who have roused kundalini (a sexual energy located in the base chakra), the crown chakra is quite warm, and the top of the head may actually soften.

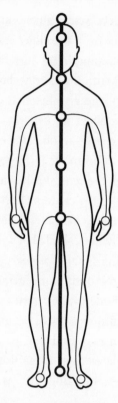

Figure 2. The energy centers and energy channels.

The brow chakra. Sometimes called the *third eye* and visualized as blue, this chakra is located on the forehead midway between your two eyes. This chakra has to do with psychic seeing, insight, dreaming, intuition, the faculties beyond consciousness. Sometimes before I do a scrying session, I touch my brow chakra with an oil or herb and say, "May I see clearly."

The throat chakra. This chakra is roughly centered in the hollow of your throat and visualized as purple. It has to do with how you communicate, how you share and receive insights, and how powerful you experience yourself as being in the world.

The heart chakra. Located in the middle of the chest between and just below the two breasts, this chakra is visualized as fiery red. This is where we sense and can change our emotions.

The solar plexus chakra. This chakra can be felt at the base of your diaphragm, in roughly the middle of your abdomen. It is yellow, the color of the warm sun. This center governs your perception of energy in the world around you.

The genital chakra. This chakra is located just at your pubic bone, and collects and shares sexual energy. This chakra can be seen as red or orange.

The ground chakra. This chakra is located midway between the feet, right along the central column. The ground chakra governs your contact with the energies of the earth, and is usually seen as green.

The brow chakra roughly corresponds with the sense of seeing, the throat chakra correlates with the faculty of sound, and the solar plexus can be thought of as governing sensation or feeling.

In addition to the main chakras, there are minor centers that permit energy to move into and out of the body. Some of the most important of these are the centers in the palms of the hands and the soles of the feet. We will be working with the energy centers in the palms when we work with the energy of objects.

We have already worked with the centers along the bottoms of the feet during energy exercises. In practice, I seldom work with the ground chakra. Usually I direct energy along my thighs to the soles of my feet rather than down the central column to the ground center. An exception to this is when I kneel back on my heels. Yogis enjoy this posture because it lines up the energies of the feet with the energies of the base and genital chakras, making a powerful foundation for moving energy.

In general magical work we will move energy along the central column from the top of the head to the feet or from the feet back up to the top of the head, rather than into or out from the chakras themselves. There are exceptions to this rule, however. For example, during sex magic we might choose to merge our chakras with our partner's chakras.

Energizing the Chakras

Do this exercise in a room where you can be alone. Stand with your feet a shoulder's width apart. Take a few deep breaths. Visualize and feel your crown chakra. See and feel white light flowing into you through the crown chakra. Slowly direct the white light downward to your brow chakra. See the blue color; feel its quality. Next, direct the white light to your throat chakra. See the purple color there and feel its quality. Now, direct the white light to your heart chakra. See the red color and feel its fiery quality. Next, direct the white light to your solar plexus chakra. See the yellow light and feel the quality of this energy. Now direct the white light to your genital chakra. See the red/orange light there and feel its energy. Now direct the white light to your ground chakra. See the green light there and feel its energy. Record your impressions.

As you move energy down the column, you might encounter a thickening, a tangle, or a block in one or more of the chakras. This indicates where you might have some issues. To clear the block:

- identify the issue;

- address the issue;

- energize the chakra.

You might immediately understand what the issue is that is blocking the chakra. If you don't, you can use your expanded senses to identify what is happening. You can do a scrying session with the question, "What is causing this block?" Before you fall asleep, you can give yourself the affirmation, "I dream about the cause of the block in my chakra."

Here are some possible issues associated with each of the chakras:

Crown chakra: **spiritual matters.** Do you have a quarrel with the religion in which you were raised? Are you uncertain of your spiritual path? You might need to make a break with old spiritual understandings, or establish a relationship with a religion or philosophy that will provide a framework for your development.

Brow chakra: **insight.** Do you doubt the perceptions you are receiving? Is the conscious mind pushing away communication from the unconscious? You might also have a physical problem with your eyes. Be gentle to them. Try cupping, an exercise to relax your eyes: Put your hands over your eyes so that the palms arch over them just like a cup. Close your eyes, and press gently with your hands on the muscles surrounding them (never directly on the eye). This can help relax your eyes and relieve headaches. You might also practice dreamwork. By approaching the images in your dreams respectfully on their own terms, you send your unconscious mind the message that you are willing to listen.

Throat chakra: **speech.** A block here might indicate that there is something you need to say that you're not permitting yourself to say. What change in your life are you resisting?

Heart chakra: **emotions.** A block here might indicate that there is a feeling you are avoiding. Are you angry? Are you in love? Are you feeling hurt or vulnerable? Once you identify the emotion and its cause, you can decide whether you need to express yourself or protect yourself.

Solar plexus chakra: **health.** How healthy are you? A block here indicates a need to pay attention to your physical well-being. You might also be blocking your psychic senses.

Genital chakra: **sexual issues.** A block here indicates that you are avoiding or misdirecting sexual energy. Are you permitting yourself to feel sexual? Are you sexually expressing energies that actually belong elsewhere, like the heart chakra?

Ground chakra: **grounding.** A block here indicates that you've cut yourself off from the earth, and from your body. You might need to learn how to feel yourself inhabit your skin again, and let yourself feel contact with the energy field of the earth.

Once you have identified your issues, you can decide how you are going to address them. This is an excellent time to make affirmations. If you are working on a block in the solar plexus, you might say, "I pay attention to my health. I eat foods that are healthy for me, I exercise, and I get enough sleep at night." You can also make affirmations in innerspace, or make a movie on your visualization screen in which you see yourself happy that you have solved those problems.

Once you have identified the issues and worked on clearing them, you can accelerate your progress by directing energy to the blocked chakras.

CLEARING BLOCKS

In a private room, stand with your feet a shoulder's width apart. Take a few deep breaths. Visualize and sense white light entering your crown chakra. Now direct the energy gently toward the blocked chakra. Feel it enter the chakra, untangling the knots and clearing the channels of energy. When the chakra is clear, see and feel the white light flowing down the central column into the ground chakra and down into the earth.

Don't force the energy through the chakra, let it gently push and gradually untangle the knotted energy threads. When you do this exercise you might get flashes of visions, feelings, or memories associated with the block. This is sometimes called *clearing junk*. This can be an intense experience! You may find that you have a lot of emotion or energy tied up in the block. Take the clearing at your own pace and don't force yourself to move faster than you can handle.

If the chakra does not clear after several sessions, this indicates a more serious problem. You might have an issue that you need to work on in therapy. Also, some blocks are simply hard-wired due to physical or emotional experiences, particularly in childhood. In that case you may send energy through the central column and simply move around the block like a stream flowing around a rock.

The energy of the body interacts with the energy fields around us. In chapter 1 we practiced drawing energy from deep within the earth and from the sun and the moon. Refining that technique, we can also exchange energy with specific places. However, it's important to notice the kind of energy in a place. Some places have a positive impact on people, while others are negative or hostile.

One way to find out about the energy of a place is to learn a little about its history. Around the world there are places that are known to be healing, particularly springs for drinking and hot springs for bathing.

There are also places that are cut off from the energy of the natural world. Big warehouse stores made of cement with no windows, positioned in the middle of large parking lots with no trees are not good places to try to exchange energy with the earth. There, it's helpful to keep yourself shielded, and it's probably also a good idea to connect with the earth again when you've left the store by doing the Mountain exercise in your front yard or neighborhood park.

Some houses capture the energies of people who have lived and died there. Haunted houses often come with stories; people who visit or live there have noticed areas of cold and have seen ghostly figures in specific places. If we inadvertently find ourselves in a haunted house, we might encounter a spirit, register sensations or visualizations, or dream about events that have occurred in the house. The spirits or energic memories in the house are often confused, and occasionally are hostile to living humans. Again, it's a good idea to protect yourself in such environments.

Few houses are as dramatic as this, however. Each home has an energy of its own, composed partly of the energy of the land on which it is built, partly of the energy put into the house by its builders, and partly of the residue of thought and emotion left by others who have lived there.

It's a good idea to investigate the energy of the place where you live. You can also try this exercise in a park.

SENSING A PLACE

Lower your shield so that your aura is freely exchanging energy with your environment. Walk around the place. Do you immediately register any feelings or images? Is there a particular place that feels different than the others?

Next, sit on a chair or bench somewhere where it's quiet. Extend your roots down into the earth. Bring the energy of the place up into your body. Do you have any feelings or images about this energy?

Then do some scrying. If you are inside, you can use a bowl of water; if you are outside, close your eyes and bring up your visualization screen. Ask the question, "What is the energy of this place?"

If you are sleeping in this place (in a bedroom in the house, or out camping), you can also induce a dream about it. Before you go to sleep, give yourself the affirmation, "I dream about the energy of this place."

Outside spaces can be tranquil, as Japanese gardens are, or wild, like a park near a waterfall. Most houses have a reasonably friendly, somewhat confused energy when we first encounter it.

In addition to sensing the existing energy, you can also generate energy fields to protect a physical space just as you use your personal shield to protect your own body.

SHIELDING A PLACE

Sit in a quiet room and center yourself. Take a few deep breaths and close your eyes. Bring up your visualization screen. Visualize the place where you live—your room, apartment, house, boat, trailer, whatever the place that is your space. Now imagine a shield of white light surrounding the space. The white light protects your house from any negative energies.

We can also put a shield up around a car, motorcycle, or bicycle. These shields will tend to fade away unless we reinforce them frequently. However, if we anchor the field to an object, it can remain solid for much longer periods of time. We will learn more about this in the next chapter.

In this chapter, we learned to create a personal shield, energize our chakras and clear blocks, investigate the energy of a place, and make a simple shield around a physical space. Next we will investigate ways to cleanse things and places that have confused or harmful energies, fill them with helpful and consciously chosen energies, and maintain energy fields around places so that they stay clean and safe.

eight

Energies of Objects

Objects come with their own energies—both those that they naturally embody, and those that they accumulate through being in specific places or being handled by specific people. Some objects, especially plants and stones, have very strong natural energy. Magicians use these in magical rites for their particular properties. Other objects are constructed specifically to contain a particular kind of magical charge. In general, when we work with an object we will clean the object of accumulated foreign energy, and charge the object with specific energy to act for a specific purpose.

Handling Objects

Before we can work with an object, we need to take a reading of its current energic state. Picking up an object and learning about its history is called *psychometry*. This is a variation of the skills we have already learned.

PSYCHOMETRY

Have a friend pick out an object for you. The object should have a bit of personal history for your friend that you know nothing about—for example, the compass he took to summer camp as a kid, or her first Barbie doll. You can take the object away and work on it in private; you don't have to do this exercise in front of your friend. Pick it up and hold it in your hand. Center yourself, take a deep breath, clear your mind, close your eyes, and bring up your visualization screen. What impressions do you get from the object? Do you see an image, or get a feeling about it? Write down your impressions. Now ask your friend about the object's history.

Psychometry is an especially helpful skill to have on tap if you are using an object you picked up at an antique shop. You may have no other source of information about the object than the impressions you get from it. Holding it in the store, you can decide whether this object is appropriate for the use you've chosen for it, or if it's better to go on searching.

All of us in our magical careers are called upon to handle an object with negative energy. The following technique is good for handling someone else's magically charged objects without either draining their energy or leaving any energy of your own on them.

THE GLOVE

Pick an object to work with. A piece of money, like a coin, is a good object for this exercise—coins pick up lots of energy from passing through so many hands.

Hold out your hand. Visualize and sense a glove of white light, much like the shield, coating your whole hand. Now pick up the object and hold it for a minute, holding the visualization and feeling of the glove. Put down the object. Reabsorb, melt away, or lay aside the glove.

Like your personal shield, this is a technique you might be called upon to use at a moment's notice. For example, if a magical friend asks, "Will you hold this tool for me for a minute?" you can use the glove to isolate yourself from the magical charge of the object, and also protect the object from picking up any of your energy.

Cleansing

Cleansing an object means stripping it of energies it has accumulated that we don't want it to have. For example, when we buy a cup in a store that we wish to use as a magical tool, we definitely want to clean it of the energies of the other people who picked it up thinking about buying it. The energy of the maker is bound into the object and can't be cleaned away, so don't buy a magical tool from someone you don't like!

Magicians usually use physical earth (dirt) and water as cleansing agents. Some magical tools, like your knife, can be buried in the earth for a period of time. Most often we'll use water for the purpose. If the object is small, like a ring, it can be immersed in the water. Larger objects can be sprinkled with water.

We can add a cleansing agent to the water. Some herbs, like lavender, work well. Most often magicians add salt to water for cleansing. Salt made from saltwater is the best cleansing agent. (If you live by the sea or ocean, you can make it by microwaving saltwater until the water evaporates and the salt is left.) Salt is not a good choice, however, if it will corrode the tool that is being cleansed, such as a knife blade.

We need to be careful how we dispose of saltwater. Salt is harmful to plants, so if we dump the saltwater out in the same place on the lawn over and over, we'll brown the grass! We also want to be careful where we throw the water, especially if we've used it to clean really negative energies from an object, so that the negative energy is properly disposed of. It's best to throw cleansing water into other water, preferably running water. (The toilet bowl will do in a pinch.)

The actual cleansing rite is very simple.

CLEANSING AN OBJECT

Fill a pretty bowl with water. Add any other cleansing agent you like to the water. Hold your hand over the water and say, "This water acts to clean and purify." Now sprinkle a little water over the object to be cleansed. You can use your hand, or a sprig of vegetation, or a honey scoop to pick up the water. As you are sprinkling the object, say, "You are cleaned and purified." Visualize and feel the confused or negative energies dissolving away from the object.

You might be called upon to work with an object that has truly objectionable energy. Some protective talismans are designed specifically to collect negative energies, and need to be cleaned out now and again. In that case you want to protect yourself from the energy of the object while you are cleansing it.

The Bracelets

Pick an object similar to the one you used in the Glove exercise. Center yourself and take some deep breaths. Now hold your arms in front of you. Visualize and feel bracelets on each arm somewhere between your wrist and halfway up your arm. You can make them any color, or see them as any metal or stone, as long as you associate that color or stone with blocking energy.

Pick up the object. Visualize and feel energy moving from the object into your hands and stopping at the bracelets. Now touch the ground with your hands. Visualize and feel the energy of the object moving into the ground.

Visualize and feel yourself taking off the bracelets. Watch and feel them melt away. Shake your hands as if shaking off water to cleanse yourself of any remaining energy from the object. Center yourself again. End with an energy-building exercise, like the Tree.

This is also a good exercise to use if you plan to heal someone. You can push energy out to the person you're touching, but none of the energy of the person washes back onto you—it is stopped by the bracelets.

In addition to cleansing objects, we can cleanse ourselves. By now we are using the shield to protect ourselves from negative environments. However, negative energy can adhere to the outside of the shield. Most of us generate or attract some negative energy as we walk through the day: someone gets angry with us, we lose our temper, or a fear crosses our mind. Cleansing returns the aura to its natural, clean state.

Cleanse Yourself

Fill a pretty, clean bowl with clear water. Sprinkle it on your head. As you do so, imagine and feel white light sheeting your aura. Give yourself the affirmation "I am clean." You can end with the Tree exercise to clean your entire energic body.

This is a great ritual to do in the bath or shower. As the water cleanses your skin, take a moment to imagine it cleaning your aura as well. You can use a cleansing agent like lavender soap to augment the action of the water, purifying your body and your energy at the same time.

You can also clean a physical space.

Cleanse a Space

First, clean the space physically by vacuuming the floor, wiping down the counters, and picking up all your stuff. This will minimize the places that negative energy can collect, such as dust bunnies and forgotten corners. When you clean your place you convince yourself that you are committed to having a clean space.

Now, walk around the house, sprinkling it with water. You can do this counterclockwise or widdershins—this is a good direction to move in when you are pushing energy out of a space. Say, "I clean this house of all negative and confused energy."

Instead of using water, you can also use a broom to chase away negative energy. Take the broom outside and shake the energy off it when done.

Charging

Once the object or space is clean, you can fill it with energy.

CHARGING OBJECTS

Pick an object you would like to infuse with energy—for example, a small box you will use to hold magical items.

To start, fill a bowl with water to cleanse the box with. Sprinkle the box with the water, saying, "You are clean." Visualize and feel the accumulated confused energies of the people who have touched it flowing away.

Light a white candle. Pass the box over the candle, saying, "You are charged to protect my stones."

Be careful not to pass the box so closely to the flame that you char it!

Now stand in front of the object. Center yourself by becoming aware of your one point. Take a few deep breaths. As you inhale, see white light flowing into your energy body through the crown center, all the way down the central column, to the ground chakra between your feet. Feel the energy return back up the central column to your one point.

Hold your hands above the object and inhale. As you exhale, visualize and sense the energy moving from your one point through your arms, through your palms, and into the box. See and feel the box completely bathed in the light.

When you feel the box has absorbed enough energy, touch the ground with your hands to wick off any excess energy. Stop pulling energy through your crown chakra and let the energy fall down your central column into the earth.

In this chapter we learned how to handle and cleanse objects and spaces, and how to charge objects and spaces with a particular energy. Next we will learn to use objects to fix energy fields around people and places.

nine

Energy for Protection

We can use our personal energy and attention to fix energy fields around ourselves, our possessions, and our homes. These shields become much easier to sustain when they are fixed to charged objects, and when we use the natural energies of plants and stones to feed into the shields.

Why would we want to protect our space magically? We do it to keep ourselves and our possessions safe from intrusion by detrimental energies and spirits. Some people balk at the discipline, or say that they wish to leave themselves and their environment open to all influences. While it is important to be able to exchange energy with our environment, it is also important to recognize that not all people and energies in this world wish us well. Warding ourselves and our space gives us the freedom to choose what energies we will interact with and what energies will pass us by.

People who have just started using magic are particularly susceptible to energy fluctuations. Before we started using magic, we weren't all that interesting to the magical world around us. Once we started using magic, however, we blipped up on the map of all the spirits and elementals and other magic users in our area. These spirits are likely to come around to investigate us. Sometimes they mean well, but wreak unintended destruction. Sometimes they mean to test us, or just to play with us. Magical protection prevents any energies from entering our space except the ones we consciously invite.

Some people who have just started using magic go in the opposite direction and see danger at every turn. Every streak of bad luck is cause to suspect a magical attack. It is true that magical practitioners do occasionally attack each other, but these occurrences are so rare that they turn into very famous stories. Magical attack takes a great deal of time and attention, and few people who have that type of discipline waste it in throwing out negative energy. If we protect our houses and protect ourselves, any energies thrown our way will bounce off harmlessly.

Magical protection is not a substitute for physical protection. Before we do anything else to our house, we need to make sure it is physically safe—that all the doors and windows lock, the smoke detectors have good batteries, and we have good electrical cords. We must also make sure that we maintain other safety procedures: staying alert as we walk around the world, paying attention to the people around us when we get cash out of a cash machine, and practicing getting into the car quickly and locking all the doors. We can also take a self-defense class. Magical protection is much more effective when it rests on a solid physical foundation.

Warding

We've taken steps to protect ourselves and protect our home. We have cleaned our aura and washed our house from top to bottom. Now we want to put up an energy shield to protect ourselves and our space. How do we do that?

The word that describes this process is *ward*. As a noun, a ward is a protective object, like a talisman or amulet. It can also be used to describe energy patterns, like pentagrams, that are applied to something to protect it. A *warden* is a magical entity that has the specific duty of protecting a given location.

As a verb, to ward means to magically protect an object or person. Warding is the act of placing magically charged objects, making energy patterns, or calling forth entities to protect a place or thing.

To ward ourselves we create our personal shield. We can augment the shield with protective objects called *talismans* or *amulets* that we carry around with us. Talismans and amulets include jewelry, medicine bags, cords, and symbols.

Pentacles are particularly popular as protection necklaces. Generally Witches wear these to identify themselves, but sometimes people who are not Witches will wear them just for the protective value. Be aware that if you are not a Witch, you might be taken for one if you wear a pentacle. Some of these come with semiprecious stones in the center. My favorite is a silver pentacle with a carnelian stone.

Some people also wear medicine bags, which are little pouches worn around the neck that contain natural objects like stones, feathers, and herbs. This is probably the best way to carry a protective object. We can also keep a stone or herb in our pocket. Specifically protective stones and plants include rowan berries, holly, onyx, carnelian, and garnet. A stone with a naturally made hole in it is an especially good protector.

Rings can also provide magical protection. A ring is an excellent personal ward because it is a circle; as it closes around the finger, it strengthens the shield that encircles the whole body. A bracelet can similarly act as a circle enhancer.

Using a Personal Ward

Do this operation in a private place where no one will disturb you.

1. **Choose the ward.** This can be a piece of jewelry, a bag, or a stone.

2. **Clean the ward.** Make sure it is energically ready to use by cleansing it with water.

3. **Clean yourself.** Sprinkle yourself with water. Do the Tree exercise.

4. **Charge the ward.** Cleanse it with an appropriate incense or touch it with an appropriate oil. Infuse the object with the appropriate colored energy. Say, "I charge this object to protect me and to sustain my personal shield."

5. **Shield yourself.** Use the shield to build your personal shield. Now put on the jewelry, or put the bag or stone in your pocket. See and feel its energy feeding into your shield.

In addition to strengthening your shield, objects worn at the chakra points can strengthen and stimulate that particular chakra. Wiccan priestesses sometimes wear moon crowns on their forehead, which stimulates the third eye for coven work. People often wear necklaces at the throat chakra and at the heart chakra. The necklace can contain a stone that has a particular energy you want to work with. If you feel that you're putting out too much energy, or that you're too vulnerable to the world, you can wear a silk scarf around your solar plexus to keep your energy to yourself. Silk is a natural energy insulator.

You can also wear objects to strengthen your minor centers. If you are doing magical bracelet work, you can augment the energy bracelets with physical ones. Just be sure to wash them periodically! Some people enjoy wearing anklets that tinkle as they walk to joyfully celebrate their connection to the earth.

I almost always have a ward with me whenever I walk around in the world. I sometimes take my wards off when I am in a natural environment that I want to sense. Some magical operations, like initiations, require you to leave all your wards behind. Most often, though, I take the wards off when I go into my own warded space. It's like letting my magical hair down.

To ward the space where you live, you must first decide how much of it you are willing or able to include. If you own or rent your own house, you can ward the entire building. It's best to ward the house and yard separately. Strangers can come into the yard (for example, the meter reader), but almost no one can come into your house unless you specifically invite them. Police and landlords are the exceptions under specific circumstances.

If you live alone in an apartment, you can ward the whole apartment, but not the building. It is neither ethical nor magically safe to ward parts of a building you do not inhabit. By doing so, you are exposing the neighbors to magical energy without their permission, and you are including their energy, which you cannot control, in your own space. Similarly, if you rent a room, you can ward only the room.

If you live in a space with other people and have no personal space of your own, you need to talk to the people you are living with about warding the space. They may or may not be magic users. They may welcome your willingness to protect everyone magically, or find it an intrusion. If you are living with people who are uncomfortable with magic, and you definitely want to ward your space, you will have to find another place to live. If you are unable to ward your space and are unable to move, you can rely on your personal shield until the day comes when you are able to control your own space.

Warding a house means energically sealing all of the entrances to the house. These include all the windows and doors. You can use a line of salt along the threshold and the window lintels. You can also put a ward above each window.

There are many types of house wards. My favorites include strings of rowan berries, and small glass eyes bought in Egyptian gift shops, which have been Arabic protection devices for many years. If you are Jewish, you can use a mezuzah over the door. You can also use a mirror to repel negative influences. Some people use horseshoes or horse brass over the door.

To get started right away, use an oven-bake clay (like Fimo) of a protective color (like red) and make small disks with holes in them to hang above the windows and doors. You can use one disk above each window or door.

PROTECTING A SPACE

1. **Clean the space.** Physically clean the house. Now walk around it counterclockwise with a broom and sweep the air. Push the unwanted energy in front of you, and sweep it out the door. You can also walk around the house counterclockwise with an egg while visualizing and/or feeling all

the vibrations from the house that are not positive for you flowing into the egg. Bury the egg outside near the front door.

2. **Shield the space.** Sit in the center of your space. Center and take a few deep breaths. Visualize and feel a shield of white light surrounding your house. Say, "This house is protected from all energies except the ones I specifically invite."

3. **Activate the wards.** Lay salt at the doors or all around the house. Draw pentagrams on all the doors and windows with your hand in the air. Put warding objects up above the doors and windows. Working clockwise, touch each of your wards in turn.

Cleaning and Charging a Warded Space

Warding a house is just like insulating it. Physical insulation keeps energy inside a house, making it warmer in the winter and cooler in the summer. Similarly, a warded house keeps negative energy outside, but it also allows energy to build up inside. All our depressed moments, fights, nightmares, and crying jags are all trapped inside our house. We'll need to periodically clean it out. Some Wiccans do this twice a year at May Day and Halloween (Beltane and Samhain). Another good time to clean magically is during a major physical housecleaning!

CLEANING A WARDED SPACE

1. **Ventilate the space.** Open all the doors and windows.

2. **Clean the space.** Walk counterclockwise around the space with a broom, sweeping unwanted energy out the door.

3. **Re-ward the space.** Close all the doors and windows. Walk clockwise around the space, touching all your wards in turn. Sit in the center of your space and visualize and feel the shield of light around your space shining bright and strong.

You can perform an abbreviated version of this rite whenever you clean the house. Just walk around the house counterclockwise once with a broom and sweep the energy out the door. If you have had a fight or a nightmare, you can also quickly sweep out that energy.

You can also take steps to control the energy in a warded space. There are two specific operations you can perform: trap the negative energy and infuse positive energy.

Objects that trap negative energy are called *tangles*. You can make a tangle out of a strip of paper (like a flycatcher) or a tangle of yarn. It's probably a good idea to make these out of something disposable. Drop the paper or yarn into a decorative jar and put it high up on a shelf. When you clean the house, be sure to take out the yarn, dispose of it outside the house, and replace the tangle.

Lots of charms generate positive energy. Sachets release pleasant scents into the air. Living plants and fresh flowers are great sources of energy, as long as they're alive and healthy; dead plants and flowers exude junky energy. Many cultures have specific good luck charms. I'm fond of wheat twists in various patterns designed to bring friendship into the house and harmony among its inhabitants. You can invoke planetary energies by placing vases of the appropriate color around the house.

Dismantling Wards

Finally, it is good magical etiquette to take down our wards when we leave a place. It's only fair to the people who will live there next. They will probably not be magic users, and have no clue what is happening when the place gets stuffier and stuffier. Even if they are magic users, it is quite hard to figure out what someone else has done to a space and break his or her wards. I've done it, and it is not fun. Also, if we leave our wards up, we leave a connection between ourselves and a place we no longer control.

CLEARING WARDS

1. **Take down the wards.** Collect all the wards from the windows and doors. Brush the doors and windows you have lined with salt to disperse the energy.

2. **Ground the shield.** Sit in the center of your space. See and feel the shield of light flowing down from the ceiling, along the walls, and into the ground.

3. **Clean the space.** Walk around the space counterclockwise with a broom, sweeping out your
   energy. Physically clean the space.

In the last few chapters we have learned how to work
with the energy field of the body, the energies of objects,
and the energy fields of places. We have cleaned them of
negativity and created positive energic charges. We have
learned how to protect ourselves and the places we live.

The next few chapters discuss ways to make our rituals
more effective by working with elements and planets, timing the ritual to take advantage of magical tides, understanding and using magical processes, and defining the
results that we want.

ten

Elements and Planets

The specific types of energy you will use most often in ritual are the energies of the elements and the planets. There are four elements and seven planets. They can be used separately or in combination.

Planets

We have already worked with earth, sun, and moon energy. The other planets in our solar system also have energies that affect the earth. One way of describing this is that the energies of the planets weave into the energy of the earth like threads in a tapestry.

This is a very ancient magic (magicians have been working with the energies of the planets since Babylonian times) and it does not belong to any particular magical tradition. Planetary energetic practices are sometimes subsumed in

113

and overshadowed by Qabalistic magic. We will not be dealing with Qabalah in this book at all, however. Instead, we will work with the ancient correspondences of the planets.

Each planet has its own energy, which was associated with a deity by the Babylonians, Greeks, Romans, and Germanic tribes. Today we still call the planets by the names of the Roman deities they were associated with. The ancient planets were also associated with colors and with metals.

Earth. The olive green of vegetation represents this power. Dark amber, rust red, and black are also used to invoke earth energy. All common stones, like granite, embody the earth. Earth brings a stable, solid energy to a magical working.

Moon. The colors silver and white and the metal silver represent this power. The moon governs the night, dreams, the cycles of the body, and spellcraft.

Mercury. The color orange represents this power, and any alloy metal that is not associated with another planet, such as brass. Mercury governs learning, herbal lore and healing, communication of any kind, and formal magic such as ritual magic.

Venus. The true emerald shade of green represents this power. Venus can also be represented by the colors pink and amber gold and the metal copper. Venus governs the power of sensuality, the enjoyment of life, and the power of deep emotional bonding and love.

Sun. The colors yellow and gold and the metal gold represent this power. The sun is the bright force that infuses our planet with life. It governs power and the ability to do what you want when you want.

Mars. The color red and the metal iron represent this power. Mars is the ancient force of war. The warrior protects, defends, and understands discipline and the appropriate use of anger. Mars represents a non-sexual passion, such as passion for work.

Jupiter. The color blue and the metal tin represent this power. Jupiter is the planet of authority, governing teaching, political office, management, and justice.

Saturn. The color black and the metal lead represent this power. Saturn governs time and fate—it is the planet of limitation and restriction.

The natural products of the earth—plants and rocks— also have been associated with planets, although these associations shift with time. If you wish to associate a rock or a plant with a planet, you can make the connection through the color of the object. Red flowers, such as crocosmia, belong to Mars, and so do red stones, like garnet and red jasper.

There are certain plants that have been used by magicians for so long that much is known about their properties.

The following are a few really useful ones that are also easy to grow or find in stores.

Aloe. The best houseplant, especially good for skin burns. Associated with the moon.

Basil. A good culinary herb; plant of Mars.

Comfrey. All-heal, boneset, good for all kinds of healing. Associated with Saturn.

Feverfew. Good for migraines and eyesight. Associated with the sun.

Lavender. Good for cleansing. A very popular herb, used in soaps and in foods. Associated with Mercury.

Rose. Rose hips are an excellent source of vitamin C, and dried rose petals are wonderful in sachets. Associated with Venus.

Sage. Another good seasoning herb, and also good to burn to cleanse the environment. Plant of Jupiter.

There are many more plants associated with the planets—an Internet search will turn up dozens of lists. This list is a good start, as these plants are very widely available.

Plants are used to make oils and incenses. You can use oils on yourself or on objects, or float a few drops in water to scent a space. Incenses can be burned to infuse an area with energy.

Earth. Pine, patchouli

Moon. Jasmine, gardenia

Mercury. Lavender, lemon

Venus. Musk, rose

Sun. Frankincense, sandalwood

Mars. Cinnamon, pennyroyal

Jupiter. Cedar, sage

Saturn. Myrrh, civet

You can easily find oils of all these scents and stick incenses of most of them as well as cones and powders to be burned on charcoal.

Magicians have also explored the properties of semiprecious stones for thousands of years. The following are a few of the most common stones, which are easy and inexpensive to buy.

Amber. A warm stone; improves general health. Associated with the sun for its color, and Venus for its friendly nature. As it is a resin, it can also be burned as an incense.

Amethyst. Protects against intoxication. In the Middle Ages, wine was served in amethyst cups to prevent the intoxication of the drinker. It is a stone of Jupiter for its color and its even-handed quality.

Bloodstone. Brings courage and strength. A stone for athletes and warriors, thus a stone of Mars. Also specifically a Witch's stone.

Carnelian. A red stone, specifically helpful in channeling energy in the energy body, and providing protection, healing, and sexual power. Associated with Mercury for its healing properties.

Citrine. A lively, energetic, happy stone. Associated with Mercury or the sun for its color.

Garnet. A protection stone and a good luck gift. Good for cleaning the blood. A Mars stone.

Hematite. Another popular protective stone. A lunar stone.

Jet. Absorbs negative energy. Female Witches, especially those in charge of groups, wear amber and jet necklaces to signify their office. Associated with Saturn.

Lapis lazuli. Jupiter's stone; embodies calm and authority.

Moss agate. Helps in grounding energy and manifesting results. Earth stone.

Moonstone. A stone of the moon for its color. Helps in foretelling the future.

Onyx. Protection, especially for travelers. A stone of Saturn.

Rose quartz. This stone of the heart belongs to Venus.

Red jasper. Helps to ground out anger, and as such, belongs to Mars.

Topaz. The stone of the sun. Brings power to anything you do.

Stones and plants contain their own energy. It's a good idea to cleanse a stone that you have bought in a store to strip it of any energy it might have picked up from people handling it.

Elemental Energy

Magical operations often use elemental forces to move energy. The four elements are earth, water, fire, and air. The ancient Greeks first identified these elements as the building blocks of our world. Each element has a different characteristic, and governs processes that affect the working.

Earth

We've already examined the earth when we talked about the planets. Earth is the most stable of all the elements and is often represented by stones. Salt can also be used in ritual to bring in earth energy. Its qualities are heavy, dark, and cool. Earth is the fleshy, mineral part of our bodies.

An earth object, like a stone or the floor of the earth itself, can be used to wick away excess energy when the ritual is complete. This is why the process is called *grounding*, or sometimes *earthing* the energy.

Earth is represented by the color green. When used as an element, the green is often brighter and closer to emerald green than the olive or pine color that represents the earth as a planet.

Process: Burying and Touching

The element of earth is used to cleanse objects and people. Witches sometimes bury knives to cleanse and dedicate them for use as a magical tool. Magicians also touch the ground or floor to ground excess energy, or to feel the comforting presence of the earth.

Water

Water is a flowing element. It has the quality of freedom. It is yielding, as a stream parts around stones, but it has great power over time, as the water will wear the stone down. Water makes up the vast majority of the human body and is essential for human survival. The color blue represents this element.

Process: Submersing and Sprinkling

The element of water is also used to cleanse objects and people. The two elements of earth and water can be combined to form a powerful cleansing agent by adding salt (embodying the earth element) to water. Objects can be completely submersed in the water. Also, water can be sprinkled on an object, place, or people you wish to cleanse.

Those things that carry the energy of the earth are generally powerful in and of themselves. Water is a wonderful carrier of energy. Often magicians will charge water specifically as a cleansing agent.

Water can be charged with the energy of the planets. Take a vase or bowl of the appropriate color (for example, red for Mars) and fill it with water. Draw red energy into your central column through your crown chakra, pull it down to your feet, bring it back up to your one point, then through your arms and out through the palms of your hands. Hold your hands over the vase and fill the water with the energy. Say, "You are charged with the power of Mars." Then you can use the water to sprinkle objects or people that you want to have the energy of Mars—for example, an iron horseshoe you plan to place over your door for protection.

Fire

Fire is the element that transmutes energy from one form to another. It is raw energy. In its most primal form it can be quite destructive. It can also be harnessed to provide heat and cook food. Fire is the energy within our bodies that keeps us going. It is represented by the color red.

Process: Burning

Fire can be a cleansing agent—for example, sometimes we will burn something we no longer want. In practical terms it is best to move the energy that we want to remove from our lives onto an easily burnable object. The easiest way to do this is to move the energy onto a piece of paper by wiping an object with the paper or by writing a descriptive phrase. Then burn the paper.

A note about fire safety: fire is the element most likely to cause an accident in the ritual circle. A few safety precautions can ensure that you always have a safe ritual. First, keep candles up on tables. Many a robe has been set afire by candles placed on the floor. If you want to put candles at the four quarters, it works well to set them on TV trays or even crates. You can cover the trays or crates with scraps of cloth of the appropriate color. Second, have an insulator beneath burning objects, in particular incense charcoal. I use a ceramic trivet tile beneath a metal dish filled with sand. Finally, when you burn something like a piece of paper, try to do it in a safe place like a sink. Ceramic is a good insulator, and a source of water is right at hand if the fire burns brighter than expected.

Air

Air is the lightest of the elements. It surrounds us; we swim in it as fish swim in the sea, often forgetting that we are surrounded by it. Air is the most important element to human survival, and we can only do without air for very short minutes at a time. Its force can be quite powerful and destructive when it rages in hurricanes and tornados. It can also be the breeze that cools us on a warm summer day. Air is represented in ritual by the color yellow.

PROCESS: FANNING AND SPEAKING

The element of air is almost always used to consecrate rather than cleanse. Air can be combined with both fire and water to accomplish a consecration.

Fire and air. A burning incense stick combines the power of fire (the flame that turns the stick into smoke) with the power of air (the smoke filling and scenting the room). You can fan smoke over an object, a place, or people. The incense can carry a planetary charge, and can also carry the energy of a particular plant. Often substances are combined in elaborate mixtures to generate energies good for cleansing, healing, or manifesting. Incense recipes are often carefully worked out and highly prized by the people who make and use them.

Water and air. This is a particularly good technique to use in places where it is impractical or forbidden to use flame. Add a few drops of an essential oil atop a bowl of water and fan the water. This distributes the energy from the oil over the object or place or person we are fanning. This is especially good for use in hospitals, offices, and other public places over which we have no direct control.

Finally, the element of air carries the words we speak over magical operations. The spoken word itself carries great power on an energic level. For that reason, it is a good idea to protect the power of our word—that is, keep our promises, and tell the truth. Each broken promise and lie weakens our ability to say magically, "This will happen." On the other hand, each promise we keep and truth we tell strengthens our own conviction that when we speak, what we say will come to pass.

Ten

In this chapter we have learned some of the correspondences of the seven planets and the four elements. Next we will take a look at magical timing, and how the hours, days, and phases of the moon affect our rituals.

eleven

Magical Timing

There are rhythms in nature that chart fluctuations in energy. Tides flow in and out. Forces wax and wane, at times swelling to great heights of power, and at other times nearly vanishing. Ritual magic becomes much easier when we time our operations to the natural cycles of energy. The patterns magicians usually work with are the cycles of the hours, the days, the lunar month, and the solar year.

Each day the earth spins around its axis, moving from sunshine into darkness. To the observer standing on the earth it appears that the sun circles around the earth, and our language still reflects this observation (e.g., we talk about *sunrise* and *sunset*). We also recognize the nodes of daylight (noon) and darkness (midnight).

Many living things respond to the sun. Certain flowers turn to face the sun as it moves across the sky. Wild baboon groups greet the sun every morning with a fairly elaborate ritual. In Hellenistic times it was very popular to pay daily respect to the sun, and that practice carries over into modern magical traditions.

When we greet the sun in the morning, we align our own energy with the energy of the planet. As the earth warms and the creatures and plants around us respond to the increasing light, there is a burst of energy available to get up and go about the day. Similarly, when the sun sets, plants close blossoms, the earth begins to cool, and day creatures settle in for a period of rest. The active forces of the day retreat and the receptive senses awaken, ready for relaxing, socializing, and dreaming.

ALIGN WITH THE SUN

At sunrise, or when you first get up in the morning, turn to the east and say, "Greeting to you, powerful sun. Infuse my day with your brightness and warmth."

At sunset, turn to the west and say, "Greeting to you, powerful sun. May your energy sustain me until I feel your warmth again."

Make this salutation even on days when it is cloudy and you cannot see the sun. Even on the darkest cloudy days, sufficient light breaks through the cloud cover so that you are able to see the objects around you, and the earth responds to the warmth and light. I have lived for many years in the Pacific Northwest where the rain clouds can persist for up to one hundred days at a time. In that case it is even more important to acknowledge the sun! I know that its energy is feeding the world, even if I don't see the bright orb.

You can perform any magical rite in the daytime or the nighttime. Some magicians prefer to work at night because it is easier to sink into the trance states that some operations require. However, if you find that you have the time to do an operation at noon, it will work perfectly well.

The other luminary in the sky, the moon, cycles through a monthly pattern (Figure 3). It gets larger and larger until it is a full circle, and then it grows smaller and smaller until we can no longer see the moon at all. These two points in the cycle are called *full moon* and *dark moon*. Some cultures and magical traditions recognize more points in the cycle, but these are the two major ones. The time between the moment the first crescent is visible in the sky to the night when the full orb is visible is called the *waxing moon*. The period between the first diminution of the orb and the night when no moon is visible at all is called the *waning moon*.

The general rule of thumb is to do rituals that intend something to increase while the moon is waxing, and do rituals to decrease things during the waning moon. In practice, if you are doing planetary magic, there are other factors that come into play. However, if you are doing a working that involves moon energy, it is wisest to take the phase of the moon into account. You can also combine the phase of the moon with another energy, like doing a planetary ritual for decrease during the waning moon.

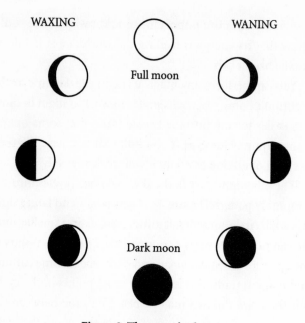

Figure 3. The moon's phases.

The moon is mostly visible at night. The sun and moon seem to trade places—one rules the day, and the other rules the night. In general you will work with the moon's power while the sun is dark, unless you are doing a lunar ritual during a planetary hour of the moon that occurs during the day.

OBSERVE MOON PHASES

Buy or locate a calendar that shows the phases of the moon. What phase is the moon in right now? When is the next full moon, and when is the next dark moon? What are the full moons that will happen this year?

There are beautiful calendars that show the sweeping arc of the moon's phases. If you buy one of these and tack it on the wall, it can help you visualize what is happening.

The moon goes through other cycles as well. It rises and sets at different spots on the horizon, swinging in a great arc from north to south and back again over a thirteen-year period. That means that we will be looking for the moon in different places in the sky. Just as we aligned ourselves with the energy of the sun, we can acknowledge the force of the moon by facing the moon and offering a salutation.

ALIGN WITH THE MOON

On seeing the first crescent: "Greeting to the silvery bow of the moon. Infuse my life with your renewal."

On seeing the full moon: "Greeting to the silvery disk of the moon. Infuse my life with your power."

On seeing the waning crescent: "Greeting to the silver orb of the moon. Wash my life clean."

At the dark moon: "Greeting to the black disk of the moon. Teach me your secrets."

Women have a regular monthly rhythm as well: the menstrual period. This is called by some the *moontime* because its pattern comes and goes like the moon. The womb sloughs its bloody lining in a process of cleansing that lasts between two and five days. Some cultures treat this as a moment of reflection; women withdraw from normal social interactions and spend a few days resting and dreaming. Some sex magic rites can only be performed by a menstruating woman.

Many cultures recognize a special power in a woman at this time. Sadly, many cultures fear this power and code it negatively, terming the process unclean. However, it is a significant power available to women that can be added to the other energies invoked in a magical rite.

Moontime Power

To learn to use this power, make a note of your cycle when you record operations in your journal. Did you feel your menstruation had any effect, such as adding energy or directing the energy in a particular way?

For myself, I learned that the first day of my moontime is entirely devoted to the renewal of the body. If I try to do any other magic during that day, the energy tends to swing wild. On the third day of my moontime, my body's energy is easy to direct, and I can add it to any rite to give it an extra charge.

The power of the sun and moon are also available as part of the set of planetary energies. These pass by cyclically in the hours of the day and the days of the week.

The Babylonians first noticed the planets, which they called the "wandering stars," and named them in the order in which they appear to an observer standing on the earth:

Saturn, Jupiter, Mars, sun, Venus, Mercury, moon. This order is encoded in the Qabalah. The farther planets—Uranus, Neptune, and Pluto—are not visible to the naked eye, and thus were not known to the ancients. Modern astrologers fold these slow-moving planets into their interpretations, but magicians generally work with the Babylonian (sometimes called *Chaldean*) order.

In Hellenistic times these planets came to be associated with the days of the week:

Sunday: sun

Monday: moon

Tuesday: Mars

Wednesday: Mercury

Thursday: Jupiter

Friday: Venus

Saturday: Saturn

Some of these associations are easy to remember in English—Sunday clearly belongs to the sun, Monday to the moon, and Saturday to Saturn. The other four days take their names from the Germanic deities associated with those planets: Tuesday is Tiw's day, Wednesday is Wodin's day, Thursday is Thor's day, and Friday is Freya's day.

You might have noticed that the days of the week do not follow the Chaldean order. This is because they were determined by a cycle of the planetary hours. Every hour of the day is ruled by a different planet in turn in the Chaldean order: Saturn, Jupiter, Mars, sun, Venus, Mercury, moon. If we list the hours of the day and the night for all twenty-four hours, we will find that a different planet starts the first hour of the day. On Sunday, it's the sun; on Monday, it's the moon.

Hour here does not mean our equal hour of sixty minutes. This was fixed relatively recently in time. Instead, there are twelve planetary hours of daylight between sunrise and sunset, and twelve planetary hours of night between sunset and sunrise. At the spring and fall equinoxes, these will be exactly sixty minutes. In the summertime, the daylight planetary hours will be longer, and the nighttime planetary hours shorter; in the wintertime, nighttime planetary hours will be longer, and daytime planetary hours shorter.

CALCULATE THE PLANETARY HOURS

If you want to calculate the planetary hours by hand:

1. Find the hour of sunrise and sunset. *Example:* 9:00 a.m. and 5:00 p.m.

2. Figure out how many minutes there are of daylight. *Example:* There are 8 hours between 9:00 a.m. and 5:00 p.m. 8 times 60 is 480.

3. Divide this number by 12 to get the number of minutes in a planetary hour. *Example:* 480 divided by 12 is 40.

4. Add the number of minutes in a planetary hour to the sunrise time to get the first hour. *Example:* 9:00 a.m. plus 40 minutes is 9:40 a.m.

5. Now add the number of minutes in the planetary hour to the result you got in step 4 to get the second hour. *Example:* 9:40 a.m. plus 40 minutes is 10:20 a.m.

6. Keep going until you have the start times for each of the planetary hours. *Example:*

Hour 1: 9:00–9:40
Hour 2: 9:40–10:20
Hour 3: 10:20–11:00
Hour 4: 11:00–11:40
Hour 5: 11:40–12:20
Hour 6: 12:20–1:00
Hour 7: 1:00–1:40
Hour 8: 1:40–2:20
Hour 9: 2:20–3:00
Hour 10: 3:00–3:40
Hour 11: 3:40–4:20
Hour 12: 4:20–5:00

7. Now do the same calculation for the hours of night. *Example:* 5:00 p.m. to 9:00 a.m. is 16 hours of night. This gives us a planetary hour of 80 minutes. Our planetary hours of night:

Hour 1: 5:00–6:20
Hour 2: 6:20–7:40
Hour 3: 7:40–9:00

Hour 4: 9:00–10:20
Hour 5: 10:20–11:40
Hour 6: 11:40–1:00
Hour 7: 1:00–2:20
Hour 8: 2:20–3:40
Hour 9: 3:40–5:00
Hour 10: 5:00–6:20
Hour 11: 6:20–7:40
Hour 12: 7:40–9:00

Now add the planets in the Chaldean order to your chart. The first hour of the day is the planet of the day. For example, hour 1, 9:00–9:40, is the hour of the sun on Sunday, the hour of the moon on Monday, the hour of Mars on Tuesday, and so on. Let's say that we calculated the planetary hours for Sunday:

Hours of daylight:

Hour 1: 9:00–9:40	sun
Hour 2: 9:40–10:20	Venus
Hour 3: 10:20–11:00	Mercury
Hour 4: 11:00–11:40	moon
Hour 5: 11:40–12:20	Saturn
Hour 6: 12:20–1:00	Jupiter
Hour 7: 1:00–1:40	Mars
Hour 8: 1:40–2:20	sun
Hour 9: 2:20–3:00	Venus
Hour 10: 3:00–3:40	Mercury
Hour 11: 3:40-4:20	moon
Hour 12: 4:20-5:00	Saturn

Hours of night:

Hour 1: 5:00–6:20		Jupiter
Hour 2: 6:20–7:40		Mars
Hour 3: 7:40–9:00		sun
Hour 4: 9:00–10:20		Venus
Hour 5: 10:20–11:40		Mercury
Hour 6: 11:40–1:00		moon
Hour 7: 1:00–2:20		Saturn
Hour 8: 2:20–3:40		Jupiter
Hour 9: 3:40–5:00		Mars
Hour 10: 5:00–6:20		sun
Hour 11: 6:20–7:40		Venus
Hour 12: 7:40–9:00		Mercury

As you can see, the next planet in the series would be the moon, the first hour of Monday.

This is a very handy calculation to be able to make. If you can do it yourself, you'll always be able to figure out the planetary hour as long as you have sunrise, sunset, and a pencil and paper. For this reason I highly recommend going through the exercise at least once. That said, if you own a computer, there are many cheap or free programs that will do the calculation for you. Also, an Internet search on "planetary hour calculation" will turn up any number of websites that will do the same thing—just enter the time of sunrise and sunset, pick the day, and get the result.

Knowing the planets of the hours and days adds power to your planetary workings. You can do a working of the moon on Monday. If you need to do a lunar working and you can't wait until Monday, you can calculate the planetary hours and do the working at the hour of the moon. If you are doing a working to improve your ability to remember dreams, that would be a working of increase, so the most powerful time to do this would be during the waxing moon, on a Monday, at the hour of the moon.

So far we have considered the cycles of the day, the week, and the month. There is also the great cycle of the year. The seasonal round charts the interaction of the earth and the sun. Spring brings longer hours of daylight and a general warming of the earth. Plants grow and animals (including humans) procreate. In the summer, trees leaf out and flowers burst into bloom. In the autumn, plants develop fruits and seeds, which animals harvest. In the winter, plants die back, and some animals hibernate. Winter is the time for the culling of the herd, when the youngest, oldest, sickest, and weakest animals die.

In the same way that we align ourselves with the daily energy of the sun, we can align ourselves with the energy of the season. In the springtime, we can note the projects that we wish to begin, and plant the seeds to manifest them. In the summertime, we use the power of the season to feed energy to our projects. In the autumn, we reap the harvest of our efforts, and pay attention to what we want to remove from our lives. Winter, like night, is a time for introspection, dreaming, and planning for the year ahead.

Gardening provides an excellent demonstration of these principles. If you garden, even if it's just to grow a few herbs in a window box, you will rapidly discover that the concept of four seasons is a pretty broad one.

In the Northwest where I live, summer is really two seasons: early summer, when the ground is warm, but we still get a lot of rain; and late summer, when the sun shines quite brightly for about six weeks. Early autumn brings a few more rain showers, but the temperature stays fairly warm and there is still a considerable amount of sun. Then, in late autumn, the days suddenly get darker and the rain sets in for the winter.

People respond to the passage of the sun across the sky and the warmth of the air, just like all other living things. Some people experience depression during the wintertime, which can be relieved by spending a few hours a day in front of a panel of lights. Most people enjoy summertime, when the air is warm and we can shed our clothes and play.

NOTICE THE SEASONS

For the next year, make journal entries on the solstices and equinoxes—roughly March 21, June 21, September 21, and December 21. Record the temperature, time of sunrise and sunset, and weather. What were you wearing? How were you feeling?

Offer a salutation to the sun: "Greeting to you, oh sun, in your passage through the year."

In spring, say: "May your renewal bring fresh joy into my life."

In summer, say: "May your strength bring power into my life."

In autumn, say: "May your resting bring cleansing to my life."

In winter, say: "May the light return!"

Almost every human culture celebrates the return of the sun at winter solstice. Christmas, Hanukkah, and the Pagan holiday of Yule fall within days of each other.

In this chapter we have learned about the association of the planets with days and hours, and the cycles of the moon and the sun. Next we will examine the processes that make ritual magic work.

twelve

Magical Processes

We've talked about the energy of the body, and the energy of place. We've examined the cycles of energy generated by the sun, moon, and planets, and how to align your magical energy with them. Now it's time to look at the processes we use to make magic happen. How does all this magic stuff actually work? There are a few rules of thumb magicians use, culled from millennia of observation and experience.

Frazer's Laws

Sir James Frazer outlined laws of magic known as *Frazer's laws* in his magnum opus *The Golden Bough*. He recognized two basic laws of magic: the law of similarity (like produces like) and the law of contagion (things that have been in contact with each other continue to affect each other); see the Find a Home ritual for an example of each. He also used the term *homeopathic magic* to describe the law of similarity, and termed both the law of contagion and the law of similarity as *sympathetic magic.*

Polarity Magic

Polarity magic operates on the principle that magical energies exist between two poles: male and female, sun and moon, day and night. Sometimes the polarities are set up in grids of equivalent energies:

male	female
sun	moon
day	night

The magical principle is that once we have defined our poles, including both of them in the ritual causes a magical energy to occur between the two poles. A man and a woman automatically generate energy; the sun and moon automatically set up a vibration between them. In practice, male and female are the poles used most often, adding the implication of heterosexual energy to the polarity.

I hasten to add that there are many pioneers, including me, who have been exploring newer ways of looking at polarity magic that include same-sex partners: young and old, white and red, or simply man and man, woman and woman. Some magical practitioners also understand that a person need not be biologically male to channel male energy, and that men can act as priestesses would in magical rites. However, we should be aware of the historical bias toward biological heterosexuality in polarity workings.

Synthema

Synthema was the term used in Hellenistic times to describe objects that had powers of the planets locked within them. Today we recognize colors, stones, plants, animals, and other objects as containing the energy of the planets. The Hellenes would assemble a number of objects containing the energy of the same planet, hoping to collect a kind of critical mass of that planetary force, or synthema. We use these principles in creating planetary workings today. For example, if I am doing a working of the sun, I might set out an altar, cover it with yellow cloth, set out six yellow candles, light amber incense, and wear a piece of gold jewelry.

Energy Return

These rules of thumb affect the construction of magical ritual. Some observations have to do with what happens to the energy once it is sent. The kind of energy that we send out into the world affects the kind of energy that we get back. What goes around, comes around. Some magicians hold that you receive an equal measure of the energy you send out. Some people, notably Wiccans, believe that whatever energy we send out comes back to us threefold, magnified by the magical act.

The Hindu word *karma* has crept into magical language. The Hindu use of this word is religious and specific, and not always well understood by non-Hindus. What it has come to mean in the West is that whatever deeds we do in this life will affect us in the next life. It also can mean that the deeds we do in this life will set up an energy vibration that will affect us in this life.

My experience is that energy I send out does return to me. Sometimes it returns with the result that I specified. Sometimes it seems to vanish and doesn't reappear for years, and then when it does, it manifests with a bang. Sometimes it comes back to me strangely—it has passed through some kind of warp and turned into something I almost didn't recognize. Paying attention to the variables of a magical operation, timing, and statement of intent have helped me identify the factors that will generate successful workings for me.

Divination

Every ritual generates patterns of energy that can be detected before and after the event. Before we do the ritual, it exists as one of the many possibilities of actions we can take. After we perform the ritual, its energy goes out into the world.

Before we perform a ritual, particularly one that we intend to make a major change in our life, it is a good idea to try to get a sense of what the probable outcome will be. We can do this by performing a divination about the operation. Similarly, after the ritual is completed, we can do a divination to figure out where the energy went.

There are many divination methods, including scrying in water, I Ching readings, and bibliomancy (opening a book and reading the first passage that you see). We don't have the space here to cover divination in detail; there are many books that cover this subject. However, we will briefly look at the most popular form of divination: the Tarot.

The Tarot is a deck of cards that contains four suits and four court cards called the *minor arcana.* Unlike other decks, the Tarot also contains a set of twenty-two cards called the *major arcana,* which presents images that represent virtues, forces, and experiences. Temperance, Strength, and Justice are virtues. The Magician, the Empress, and the High Priestess are forces. The Hanged Man, the Tower, and the Lovers are experiences. Some interpretations of the major arcana say that the cards tell a story about one person's journey through successive states and experiences— from the bold innocence of the Fool, through the training of the Magician, the formative initiatory experiences like the Hanged Man, adversity like the Tower, through to the fulfillment of the World.

One of the most popular decks, especially for people just starting to use the Tarot, is called the Rider-Waite deck. This was the first deck that provided images for all the suit cards, as well as the court cards and major arcana, which simplified the task of interpreting them. The deck was designed by Arthur Edward Waite and drawn by

Pamela Colman Smith. It is available through U.S. Games in several versions, including a thimble-sized carry-in-your-pocket variety. It comes with a booklet explaining the meaning of the cards.

There are many, many decks available through U.S. Games and other companies. Some are simple and some are quite complicated. If you choose to obtain a Tarot deck to use for divination operations, you can look at several and choose the one that seems to best fit your temperament. As you use the cards, you will almost certainly find that you will outgrow your first deck and move on to a more complicated deck, or expand into collecting several to use in different moods.

Getting to Know Your Deck

Take the deck out of its box. Lay out the major arcana on the floor, from the Fool to the World/Universe. Look at each card in turn. Do you see a story in the cards?

Lay out the minor arcana one suit at a time. Look at all the disks from the Ace to the King. Then look at the cups, swords, and wands. Do you see a theme in each of the suits?

A note about handling Tarot cards: traditionally they are considered to be very sensitive to touch. Serious readers usually handle their cards very scrupulously. It's best to buy a deck that is shrink-wrapped—that is, one that no one has touched. Most shops will offer one deck for viewing, and sell you a deck that hasn't been opened. You will almost never see Tarot decks offered secondhand, and these are best used for research purposes only and not for readings. The deck will stay both neat and energically stable if you keep it wrapped in a cloth, especially an energically insulating cloth like silk or wool or linen.

DOING A READING FOR A RITUAL

Take your cards out of their cloth. You can do the reading on the cloth if you like. Shuffle the cards, thinking the question you wish to be answered: "What will be the result of this ritual?" Cut the deck and lay out three cards. Look up the meaning of the cards in your booklet.

You can do this reading with a single card. Using three cards gives the Tarot a chance to talk about more than one force involved in the ritual. Usually the relationship of the three cards is very clear. For example, if you are doing a ritual to attract love, you might draw the Ace of Cups (the force of love), the Two of Cups (love shared with another), and the Lovers (the cosmic force of bonding and attraction), indicating that the ritual is likely to be quite successful. You might draw a sword card indicating some conflict in yourself about the ritual. You might also draw a major arcana card indicating that forces outside yourself are affecting the reading.

Each deck of cards comes with a small booklet interpreting the meaning of the cards. Many also have accompanying books that explain the deck in more detail. The same cards in different decks may mean different things. For example, the Seven of Swords in the Motherpeace deck has a different meaning than the Seven of Swords in the Thoth deck. It's important to get to know each deck individually as well as the Tarot in general. Your own interpretations based on your experience with the cards is always the best source of information for you.

The Pyramid

The magical pyramid is composed of four sides: knowledge, will, courage, and silence. These qualities all refer to the character of the magician who is doing the ritual. These are the intangible qualities essential to making a magical rite work.

Will is a carefully chosen word. For a ritual to work, it isn't enough to wish, or vaguely desire, or be ready to accept the outcome—you must passionately require the ritual to work. Will also means bringing the discipline to the rite that will make it happen: doing magical exercises to increase skill, learning magical processes, and assembling the raw materials.

Knowledge means visualization (being able to imagine the result), creativity (generating lots of ideas for making the rite work), and understanding.

Courage means that you have confidence in yourself and in your work.

Silence means do not talk to people about magic in progress. If you've done a ritual to get a job, don't brag about it to friends—don't even mention it until you have a job and the ritual has been successful. Then you can talk to others about it. One reason for this is that talking about the magic has a tendency to dissipate its energy—it gets directed into the conversation instead of making the result happen. Another reason is that the people you talk to may cut into your faith in the rite. "The economy is so bad, how on earth is a ritual going to counteract that?" Silence gives the ritual the space and time it needs to generate its results.

In this chapter we have learned some of the processes involved in making rituals work. Next we will figure out how to get the ritual results we want.

thirteen

Ritual Results

The very first step in doing a ritual is to figure out why we are doing the rite. Up until now every exercise in this book could be done for practice, although every one also has a positive result. Now we will work with rituals designed for a specific magical purpose.

Statement of Intent

When we do a ritual, we must determine the result we wish the ritual to have—the specific direction we wish to send the energy of the rite. It is most effective to frame that result in a statement of intent, which is spoken during the rite. This is really the core of performing ritual magic.

We have talked about the three rules of writing affirmations:

- Use the present tense.

- State the positive result, not the negative.

- Specify what, not how.

These rules also apply to creating a statement of intent. In general, it is best to limit it to a single line. If you can't say what you want to do in one sentence, then you probably need to think about what you are trying to do. Especially in the beginning, you will have the most success if you keep it simple and work for one result at a time. Later, when you have done some simple rituals, you can work for more than one result with the same ritual energy.

Once you have decided on the ritual purpose and formed it into a single sentence, it is a good idea to write it down on a piece of paper so that you can read it during the ritual. Especially at first, there are many things to keep track of as you do a ritual. If you write down the statement of intent, you won't have to remember it and you can simply read it at the appropriate moment.

Also, writing down the statement of intent in advance lets you take your time figuring out exactly what you want to say.

Types of Results

The most popular reasons to perform rituals fall into four basic categories: manifesting prosperity, relationships, health, and spiritual advancement.

Manifesting prosperity has to do with material wealth. Many rituals involve getting a new or better job. We might need an influx of cash, or something specific, like a car. Everyone needs a place to live, so finding a place to rent or closing a house sale deal are also on the list.

The basic rule about manifesting prosperity is that you must follow up your magic with physical action. If you do a ritual to get a new job, and you never look at a newspaper or ask your friends who's hiring, you are much less likely to be successful! Magic is not a substitute for action in the world. It supplements our efforts, adding energy and steering our energy in the direction most likely to be successful.

Sometimes magic does make things happen that we really need to happen right now, like an influx of cash to pay an unexpected bill, or a really good deal on a car. However, if you find yourself using emergency magic on a regular basis, that's a sign that you need to reassess how you are living your life. Do you need to make more money? Maybe a better job is in order. Or is it just that you need to learn to budget the money you already have? Budgets are definitely not fun, but they are tools that permit us to get what we want!

This principle also holds for relationships. If you perform a ritual to find a lover or to generate friends and then you don't socialize, the ritual has no chance to function. Throw the energy into the world, then follow up! Place a personal ad, join a club, take a class, or even hang out in a bar.

We've already spent some time talking about health and how to maintain it. Even the healthiest person stumbles now and again: a virus takes us down for a week, or a fall breaks a bone. These are acute and nonrepeating health problems. In our times there are also a number of diseases that are chronic and uncurable, some of which are fatal and some of which are not. Magic can help to cure an acute problem and to stabilize a chronic one. Magic is especially good at providing an influx of energy to keep our bodies going.

There is a whole category of magical result that can be termed spiritual. You might find a need at some point in your life to reassess what you've been doing. Perhaps you're in the wrong job, the wrong marriage, or perhaps you just need to pay attention to parts of yourself that you have been neglecting. You can focus your magic toward starting a new endeavor.

You might also feel the need to explore a religion, celebrate life's passages, or connect with a deeper sense of purpose. A magical ritual can help you begin the search for a new spiritual path.

Future-Pacing

Future-pacing is a term that comes from Neuro-Linguistic Programming. Now that you know what you want, imagine that you have gotten it. What does your life look like? How do you feel? What do you think about your life now that the ritual has happened? Visualize yourself walking through your day and sense the feelings that you have.

Is your life better because of the ritual? Is there an unintended consequence that you dislike? If your future-pacing turns up a side effect that you want to avoid, go back to your statement of intent and restate it. Then future-pace the result again. Continue through this process until you can imagine yourself happy with the result of your ritual.

There is a magical truism: "Be careful what you ask for—you might get it." This is pointing out the danger that the result you work for might have unintended side effects. If you do a ritual to be beautiful to everyone who looks at you, you will rapidly discover that there are people you don't want looking at you! Future-pacing helps you catch those side effects and prevent them before they happen, and it helps you shape your statement of intent to get exactly what you want.

Have Faith in the Rite

Once the ritual is completed, act as if the rite has been successful. If you think you made a technical error during the rite, you can note that in your journal. However, don't fret about it ("Ohmigosh, I forgot to call the water quarter! I'm sure it won't work!"). And try not to anxiously watch the world for signs of success like a kid waiting for a package in the mail ("Is it here yet?"). The best thing to do when you've finished a ritual is to go about life calmly, secure in the knowledge that the ritual's result is in the process of manifesting. Trust your magic.

There's a nice feedback loop that gets set up when you do this. As you have more and more successful rituals, you get more used to doing a rite and then walking away reassured. Magic becomes more and more a part of how you live your life.

Assessing the Results

When you have performed the ritual and recorded what you have done, give it some time to work. The amount of time will vary depending on the magnitude and complexity of the result you are working toward. A ritual for quick money should bring results within a few days; a new job or relationship will take longer.

At some point it should become clear that the ritual has worked, or that it has not worked. If you got a result, record that in your journal also. It's very useful to go back over your past rituals and notice the successes. If the ritual did not bring the result you wanted, go back and examine your notes about the rite. Did you clearly form your statement of intent? Were you too specific? ("I want a relationship with a six-foot-five, 36-22-36 redhead.") Were you not specific enough? ("I want a relationship.") An overly detailed statement of intent has a reduced chance of success, while an overly general intent is dangerous, as it leaves a lot of room for interpretation. Did you really mean to adopt a zoo animal or end up in Big Brothers and Sisters, or did you want a *romantic* relationship?

Another thing to examine is the correspondences. Did you use moon attributions for your new relationship ritual? It all seemed so wonderful, just like a dream, and then suddenly it vanished and the relationship was over. You're better off using Venus, or even the sun, to work for a relationship that will last in the long term. However, if you're interested in a fling, the moon may be just the thing!

If you still can't figure out why the ritual didn't work, you can turn to divination. Do a Tarot reading with the question, "Why did my ritual fail to give me what I asked for in my statement of intent?" Pull three cards. This should give you a new perspective and some ideas about new directions to go in. Perhaps you did a ritual for a relationship when what really occupies your mind is getting a new job. Take care of the job first, and then you can relax and contemplate love.

It could also be that you are pushing too hard. You have wanted this thing for a long time, you're frustrated, and nothing seems to happen. You can get stuck in a place where you're pushing energy at the frustration instead of the intended result of your ritual. If you've been doing a set of workings and they seem to be going nowhere, put that particular set of rituals aside and work on something completely different. Start with something you are already pretty good at. If you make friends easily, do a ritual to make new friends. When you have a ritual success or two under your belt, that can help calm you down and bring confidence into your ritual work. Your attitude toward the working is the most important part of the ritual; expect success and you'll get it!

Dare to Dream

Many rituals are focused on immediate, practical results. You need to pay an unexpected bill right away, or you need to heal yourself, or you need a place to stay or a job. Rituals can also work for long-term goals. Take a moment to think about what you really want in your life. You can't get what you want if you don't know what that is.

Take a moment to dream. Forget about what is practical, what you think you might be able to pull off, what you can afford, what your parents will approve, or what you thought you wanted when you were five. If you could wave a magic wand and have anything at all in the world, what would that be? Where would you live? What job would you do? Who would your friends be? What adventures would you be having?

Just admitting to yourself what you really desire is the first step toward achieving it. As you continue to think about what you want to do, it becomes clear what keeps you from doing it, and what steps you need to take to make it happen. Once in a while, when you get a free wish—like when you see a shooting star—wish for your wildest dream.

In this chapter we learned how to specify the ritual result. Next we will explore creating ritual space.

fourteen

Ritual Space and Tools

There are three things that differentiate the ritual magician from someone who only casts spells. The first is knowledge. We magicians know why we are doing what we do. We know correspondences, we know the spell sources, we understand the processes behind the operation. The second is practice. Magicians approach operations consciously, build skills with discipline, and work with energy systematically. The third is place. Magicians create ritual space in which to perform magical operations.

The Circle

Magicians have been creating ritual space for many thousands of years. Ritual space is a special kind of warded space. We use the same techniques to create ritual space that we do to ward our living space. However, a house ward is both permanent and somewhat permeable—people and pets enter and leave the house. A ritual circle, on the other hand, is like an airtight room: it is designed to completely hold out all other energies and completely hold in the energy that is invoked into it for a limited period of time. This hermetically sealed chamber allows the magician to concentrate energy and direct it to a specific purpose.

A ritual space can have religious significance. Many Pagan religions work with the magic circle. Native American tribes create medicine wheels, and Buddhists create mandalas. The ritual space can effectively include religious symbols to invoke the energy of spirits or deities or just the energy of the religion itself to help create the space.

However, ritual space need not have a particular religious focus. Magic texts have described the creation of circles for many thousands of years. Today, ceremonial magicians often engage in rituals with a philosophic rather than religious basis.

Mandala of Space

A ritual space defines a model of the world. It is essentially a world in miniature—a sphere or mandala. To create this energy structure, we need a framework to hang it on. The framework used most often by many cultures around the world is defining the four cardinal directions: north, south, east, and west.

Every magical tradition makes particular associations with the directions. The most fundamental, and the one that is common to almost all of them, is the association of direction and element. The ancient Greek philosophers first described these elements as the basic building blocks of the world. This four-element idea traveled very far around the world. Today, we can find elements in Hindu religion, as well as threaded throughout Western philosophy. The associations are:

East: air

South: fire

West: water

North: earth

This does not describe any particular physical place. For example, if you live on the east coast of the United States, east is still the magical direction of air, even though in the physical world there is an ocean in that direction. These associations describe an ideal, mythical space.

The symbols we used in the Seeing Shapes exercise work well to represent the elements of the directions: the yellow diamond represents air and east, the red triangle represents fire and south, the blue circle represents water and west, and the green square represents earth and north.

In addition to the four quarters, the magician can call upon the sky above and the ground below. The sky is associated with the luminaries (the sun and moon), and with the stars at night—the vast panoply of space stretching above us. The ground is the earth—not as an element, but as the world within which we live, including all the elements. At the center stands the magician.

Ritual Tools

The tools we will use for the rituals in this book are simple household objects. There are specific tools that ceremonial magicians and Witches use for their rites, such as a ceremonial knife or a cup, or metal talismans inscribed with sigils. However, we will not need any of those to accomplish our tasks. There are no particular requirements about size, shape, or color, and we will not be consecrating the tools or marking them with signs.

You can use the items you already own to do any magic in this book. The most important thing is to get started now! Later, as time and money permit, you can start stocking your magical tool chest.

That said, when you get the time and money, it is preferable to have special tools that you use only for rituals. This keeps the energy of the object clean, so that you don't have to cleanse it each time you do a ritual. An object can also accumulate magical energy over time. Finally, if you have separate tools to do magic and you keep them together in a specific place, you always know where they are when you want to do a ritual!

The tools listed here are easily available and inexpensive, so it will be fairly easy to assemble the set, whether you're raiding your cupboards or making a trip to the store.

Broom

It is best to buy a new broom. If you need to use a broom you already own, do clean the straw before you use it. Brooms accumulate physical as well as psychic dirt that you do not want to bring into your ritual. Craftspeople also make special decorative brooms with carved handles and colored straw that are excellent for this purpose.

Once you have bought your magical broom, do not use it for sweeping floors, and keep it in a separate place from your everyday brooms. The broom is used for sweeping out negative energy, cleaning a space you will use for ritual, and for laying across a door when you want to protect it magically.

Bowl

Many rituals require water, which means having a container to hold the water. Again, you can use any bowl in your kitchen. However, it is very nice to have a special bowl you use only for ritual purposes. This can be made of clear glass, blue glass, or blue ceramic. All of these carry the association of water. You can choose another color if you like—there's no hard-and-fast rule here. However, especially if you're new to magic, it's nice when your tools reinforce the association you're building with the element.

The bowl is used to cleanse items, cleanse the ritual space, and bring the element of water into the ritual.

Incense Burner

The kind of incense burner or censer you have depends on the kind of incense you use. If you plan to burn charcoal and powdered incense, you'll want a fireproof dish at a minimum. Make sure to use an insulator either in or under the dish. I use a deep metal dish filled with sand and place this on a ceramic tile. When the rite is complete, the charcoal is often still burning, so I place the entire dish in the sink until the charcoal is cold.

For most rituals, stick or cone incense is perfectly acceptable. I like to collect small stick incense packages from Indian gift shops—these come in many different scents, so I can have at least one incense on hand for each of the planetary attributions. Stick incense burners come in several kinds. Some brands of incense actually come with their own little burner: a small ceramic tile into which you insert the incense. There's also another kind that is flat and narrow with a curve up at the end. You put the incense into a hole at the curved end, so that it is suspended over the flat section. This kind of incense burner catches the ash, which makes cleanup easy.

Similarly, there are many kinds of incense burners that hold cones. I have one on my house altar that is shaped like a little house—the smoke comes out the chimney! This is great for house protection and expansion rituals.

Incense consecrates magical tools and brings the joined elements of fire and air into a ritual.

Candles

Votive candles are very inexpensive, and so are votive candleholders. You'll need at least two candleholders and a selection of candle colors: white, black, yellow, red, blue, and green, at least. If you find a really good collection you can also add orange, silver, and gold. Look for orange and black votives at Halloween in particular.

Tapers require candleholders and come in many different sizes. Be sure to get the size of holder that matches your taper. Pillar candles usually stand by themselves and burn down the center of the pillar, forming their own holder. You can use these if you want to bring a special charge to a ritual.

Some people prefer to use beeswax candles for their scent and for the natural quality of the wax. Beekeepers often sell beeswax candles at craft fairs and farmers' markets. These come in tapers, and less often as votives or tea candles. These can be used in addition to planetary and elemental candles, or in rituals that don't involve planetary or elemental energies. Some magicians like to use a single beeswax candle in the back center of the altar as a symbol of light and for physical illumination.

Tea candles usually come just in white. They have the added advantage of coming with their own candleholders! These are excellent to use if you need a lot of candles.

Candles bring the element of fire into a ritual. The color of the candle can invoke the energy of an element or of a planet.

Pen and Paper

Medieval magicians paid a lot more attention to pen and paper than we do now, partly because they were so much harder to come by. If you like the historical feel of it, you can use an ink pen to write your statement of intent. I used one when I was starting to do magic. It helped to bring the right sense of seriousness to the venture. It was also pretty messy, though, so I eventually switched to ink cartridge pens, which I still use.

You can use any paper you like. If you can get a nice paper, like linen or parchment, it looks especially good with flowing ink. If you are doing a planetary or elemental working, you can use paper of the color of the energy you are invoking. However, lined notebook paper and a ballpoint will also work.

Space Markers

You might decide to visually mark your circle. I have used salt (had to vacuum it up!), chalk (messy to clean up), tape (time consuming), yarn (a bit hard to work with as it's thin), and cotton rope (introduced to me by a friend recently, and my favorite material). I found that the rope responded more easily to me after I washed it.

Altar and Cloth

Any small, portable table will do for an altar. I often use an inexpensive wooden TV tray. I cover this with a brightly colored woven place mat from Mexico. I also use felt from the craft store and scraps of cloth from the fabric store.

Tool Storage and Permanent Altar

You will need a place to store your magical tools. Some people use chests or boxes to store their magical items. Others use a stand-alone bookshelf unit. This has the added bonus of providing a top shelf for an altar.

In addition to the temporary altar you set up for your rituals, you will probably eventually want to set up a permanent altar. This is the place where you keep items that are currently being used in rituals. You might keep your bowl and incense burner there. Also, items that are used in a series of rituals or that still carry the energy of a ritual that's in the process of manifesting might end up there. For example, you can set up a candle for a particular purpose and light it several nights in a row.

The permanent altar can be any surface at all. My current altar is a single wall-mounted bookshelf. You can place a beeswax candle on it if you like. Any item that you feel is magical, like a stone or a flower, might end up there. Just keep it neat!

In this chapter you learned how to create ritual space and use magical tools. The rest of this book provides you with examples of rituals you can do.

The Rituals

In the following pages, there are a number of rituals that use the powers of the elements and the planets, magical processes, and magical timing to accomplish specific, real-world results. The first section is a ritual outline, which will help us prepare for the ritual, create the circle, perform the working, and close the rite. Where the outline says "Perform the working," insert the actions from the "Ritual Action" section in each of the following rituals.

All of these rituals are tested and will work. However, any creativity you can add to the rite will greatly enhance its effectiveness for you. Experiment with writing your own quarter callings, change the elements or the planets, and try different incenses and oils. If you have done the exercises in this book, you have all the knowledge and skills you need to reshape each of these rites into a form that will work for you or to create your own rituals.

Each ritual includes a suggestion for both an elemental and a planetary energy to work with to accomplish the ritual purpose. You can use either the element or the planet, or you can choose to use both energies. If you are using an altar cloth, you can use white, one of the colors, or both of the colors—just drape the elemental altar cloth on half of the altar, and drape the planetary cloth on the other half. You are also free to use other planets or elements if you like.

None of the possible combinations of planetary and elemental attributions repeat. However, not all are represented in this collection of rituals. You are free to experiment with the combinations—both the ones used here and the ones not represented—to create your own rituals.

Please note that earth is both an element and a planet. There are no combinations of elements with the planet earth here. However, whenever earth shows up in a ritual, there is a suggestion to use an incense of earth as well as an incense for the planet to honor its crossover status and bring an extra charge into the rite.

You can use the color white in place of any of the planetary colors. You can assemble a set of elemental colors—yellow, red, blue, and green—and use these plus white to cover the planetary colors, substituting white for both the moon (silver) and Saturn (black). The full spectrum of planetary and elemental colors would be: green (earth and Venus), silver (the moon), orange (Mercury), yellow (air and the sun), red (fire and Mars), blue (water and Jupiter), and black (Saturn).

The Ritual Outline

Prepare for the Ritual

Before you create a ritual space, you must make the preparations for the ritual. As with any serious enterprise, if you plan what you want to do before you do it you have a much higher chance of success.

DEFINE THE PURPOSE

Choose and define the result that you want. This book contains many examples. Chapter 13 covers how to construct a statement of intent to read during the ritual. Write this down, preferably in a single sentence.

SET THE TIME

Next, choose the day and time you will be doing the ritual. You can do any ritual at any time. Consider that days and hours harmonize with planetary energy, and the phase of the moon can be coordinated with the type of working.

Choose a time when you can physically perform the ritual. You might need to work around other people's schedules to ensure you will have use of the space where you will perform the ritual. You might also take into consideration the magical timing of the sun, moon, or planets. Chapter 11 discusses these in depth.

CHOOSE YOUR ENERGY

Decide on the type of elemental and planetary energy you will use. Check the correspondences for this type of energy.

Chapter 10 explores colors, plants, and metals associated with the planets and elements.

DO A DIVINATION

Once you've set the purpose and chosen a time, it's a good idea to do a divination. Chapter 12 covers divination.

If you are using Tarot as your divination tool, pick up your deck, shuffle it while asking, "What will be the result if I do this ritual?", and pick a single card. If the card is disastrous, pull two more cards to clarify the answer. If they remain negative, cancel the rite. If the card points out a problem, go back to your statement of intent and rewrite it to solve the problem, then do the divination again. If the card is favorable, you may put it on the altar for the working. You can also choose a card that represents the outcome you desire and place it on the altar.

PHYSICAL PREPARATIONS

Physically prepare for the ritual. Choose the room where you will perform the ritual. If you have a space that is your own, such as a bedroom or living room, that is the most logical place to do the rite. However, any space will do as long as it is private and you feel good about the energy in the space. Do not make yourself do a ritual in a space you have qualms about just because it is available to you at the right time! The best magician can do magic in any location with the right energy.

It is more effective to perform magical rites in spaces that are physically clean. Pick up any objects strewn around and vacuum or mop the floor. Also, make sure that you yourself are physically clean. Did you last have a shower a few hours ago or was it last week? If you don't have time for a shower, you can brush your teeth and comb your hair.

Next, assemble all the objects you will need for the ritual. This includes any tools you will use, such as your broom or a bowl of water, candles (don't forget matches), and documents, including your statement of intent, as well as the ritual outline and words. For elaborate rituals, you can make a list of the things you will need and consult it as you are preparing the space.

DEFINE THE SPACE

Next, physically mark the space you will be using. You might use a string or rope to make a circle on the floor. It is also a good idea to place objects at the four quarters. You can use the posters you made in chapter 3 of the yellow diamond, red triangle, blue circle, and green square. One very popular technique is to use colored candles or candles in colored containers—this has the handy side effect of increasing the light in the space!

SET UP THE ALTAR

Place a table in the center of the space. It looks nice if you drape the table with a cloth. You can choose a cloth of the color corresponding with the planet or element you are working with. Place the tools on it that you will use in your ritual: candles, bowl of water, incense, oil, your statement of purpose, and any special tool you may be using.

You might put your broom next to the altar and add altar candles that will provide lighting for you to see by.

Create Ritual Space
Light the altar candles.

Center Yourself
Stand in the center of the space and face the table. Most magicians face east, the direction of the rising sun, and start and end all actions in the east. Center yourself; do the Mountain exercise or the Tree exercise and do a breathing exercise.

Magical Cleansing
Clean the space energically. You can walk counterclockwise around the circle with a broom, or you can sprinkle the space with water. Say:

> "This space is clean for the purpose of my rite."

Quarter Invocation
Now invoke the quarters. Face each direction in turn and say a small invocation. If you have used candles, you can light them when you say the invocation.

> "I call on the powers of the east to protect
> this space while I perform this rite."

> "I call on the powers of the south to protect
> this space while I perform this rite."

"I call on the powers of the west to protect
this space while I perform this rite."

"I call on the powers of the north to protect
this space while I perform this rite."

Turn back to the east and say:

"I call upon the powers of great space above to
protect this space while I perform this rite."

"I call upon the powers of the world below to
protect this space while I perform this rite."

CREATE THE SPHERE

Standing in the center of the circle, visualize and feel a
sphere of white light growing around you. It starts at a
point beneath your feet, flows up like a bowl to touch the
four quarters, and flows back together again to a point
above your head. Say:

"Above me, below me, all around me,
The sphere encloses and protects me
While I perform this magic rite."

Perform the Working

Next fill the space with energy. Starting in the east, walk
around the circumference of the circle. You can visualize
white light, or light the color of a planet if you are invoking a planetary energy. Say:

> "This circle is filled with a vortex of power
> to accomplish the purpose of this rite."

Now read your declaration of purpose. Perform the ritual action you have decided to do.

DISASSEMBLE THE RITUAL SPACE

When you are finished, face each of the quarters in turn—east, south, west, north—and say:

> "I thank the powers of the east for protecting
> this space while I performed this rite."

> "I thank the powers of the south for protecting
> this space while I performed this rite."

> "I thank the powers of the west for protecting
> this space while I performed this rite."

> "I thank the powers of the north for protecting
> this space while I performed this rite."

Standing in the center of the circle, visualize and feel the sphere collapsing again from the point above your head, down through the quarters, to the point beneath your feet. Say:

> "Down, down, energy ground."

CLEAN UP

Put your physical objects away. Pour out the water on the ground. Extinguish the incense and candles. Put all your tools away. Bury or burn any objects that you used to clean negative energy.

Post-ritual

Record the working in your journal. When sufficient time has passed, assess the effects of the ritual. If necessary, modify the ritual and do it again.

Outline for Creating Ritual Space

Define the purpose

Set the time

Do a divination

Clean the space

Set up the altar

Invoke the quarters

Erect the energy sphere

State the purpose

Circumambulate to create an energy vortex (or use any other energy-generating technique you are familiar with)

Perform the working

Thank the quarters

Ground the energy sphere

Record the working

Assess the results

Find a Home

You need a place to live *now!* You're moving out from home for the first time, you can't stand your roommates, your basement flooded and you're tired of the mildew—for whatever reason, you can't stay in this place a second longer. This is the ritual for you.

At one point I was living in a group house (a place with a lot of roommates) that was folding. Our one-year lease was up and we weren't going to renew it. We had a month to find a new place. Three of us in the house had decided to continue to live together. We did the desired result exercise, set up the altar, and spoke our statement of intent together. Then we went house-hunting. When we found the perfect house, we knew it immediately. We competed with fifteen other people for that house and we got it! We even moved in on schedule too.

It could be that you're at the place in your life where you want to stop paying rent and buy your own house. This ritual will work for that purpose too. If you're working to buy rather than rent a place, give the ritual a little more time to work.

Desired Result

Ask yourself the following questions: How much can you afford to spend on a place to live? Is the most important thing to keep the rent cheap and get the most you can for your buck, or is there some flex in your budget?

Who will you be living with? Do you prefer to live by yourself, do you intend to rent rooms out, or do you want to rent part of a space from someone else? Are you doing the ritual on behalf of your entire family? Even if the people you plan to live with aren't going to do the ritual with you, it's best to discuss the statement of intent with them so that their wishes aren't working against the ritual result.

How big do you need the space to be? Are there any special qualities you are looking for—room for a garden, a location close to the bus lines, or a great view? Here are the items to cover in your statement of intent:

- Amount you can pay for a place (cheap, inexpensive, moderate, reasonable, doesn't matter)
- Who will live there
- Size of space and special qualities

For example:

> "I live in a cheap, quiet room with
> quiet, respectful roommates."

"I live in an inexpensive apartment near
the bus lines with a great view of a park."

"I buy a reasonably priced, roomy house with
bedrooms for everyone and a safe yard for the kids."

"I live in an impressive penthouse
with a view of the city."

Ritual Specifics

Elemental energy: earth

Planetary energy: Jupiter

Timing: Sunday, Thursday, any hour of Jupiter, waxing
moon/full moon

Altar cloth: blue or green

Candles: white, blue, or green

Incense: pine, and cedar or sage

Special Tools

For this working you will need a small representation of a
house. Some ideas include a small toy house, a house that
takes a tea candle so that it looks as if it's lit from within,
or an incense burner in the shape of a house. This operates on the law of similarity.

If you have your heart set on living in a particular
neighborhood, pick up a rock or a scoop of dirt from the
neighborhood. Set the stone or dirt near or beneath your
model house. This uses the magical process of contagion.

Ritual Action

If you have candles, light them. For earth, light a white or green candle and say, "I invoke the power of earth." For Jupiter, light a white or blue candle and say, "I invoke the power of Jupiter."

Light the pine incense from the earth candle. Light the cedar or sage incense from the Jupiter candle. Holding the incense burner or sticks of incense in your hand, walk clockwise once around your circle, saying, "This circle fills with a vortex of energy to accomplish this rite."

Read your statement of intent. If your model house has a candle or incense, light it. Go into your innerspace and imagine yourself walking through the door of your perfect home.

Ritual Follow-up

Place the model house on your permanent altar. Now do the normal follow-through: read the paper, talk to a realtor, do the real-world stuff necessary to find your new home.

When you move into your new place, place your model house on your house altar, fireplace mantle, or kitchen windowsill as a reminder of the magic that brought your house into your life. You can include your model house in your home warding and blessing rituals.

Get a Job

You need a new job. You were laid off from your last one, you just graduated from school, you've been a homemaker, or you're just plain tired of what you have been doing and need a change. It's time to put your magic to work!

Desired Result

Instead of focusing on a specific job, like housekeeper or manager or software tester, think about what you want from a job.

> **Time.** What hours do you want? Must you have weekdays, or will any time do? Do you want a part-time or full-time job?
>
> **Money.** How much money do you want to make?
>
> **Benefits.** How important are health and retirement benefits to you? Is this a higher priority than schedule or money?
>
> **Autonomy.** Do you want a job where you work by yourself, a job with other people in a team, one where

your manager supports you, or a place where you decide what you do each day?

Other needs. Some people love to travel, while others will never travel. Some jobs provide a vehicle to drive. Some jobs include access to the services the job provides, like dental care or legal advice.

List each of your desired results in priority order to generate your statement of intent. For example:

> "A job that makes a lot of money, with a lot of autonomy, good benefits, and some travel."

> "A job that pays great benefits, on weekdays only, working with a team, and makes a decent wage."

Write a Magical Resume

Put your name and address on the top, phone, and e-mail address if you have one. Next, boldface the word *Objective*, but instead of writing the usual blurb here (like "I am looking for a job in sales with an opportunity for advancement"), put in your statement of intent.

Boldface the phrase *Job History*, and list your jobs for the last five years, the dates you worked, and your job title. There, instead of writing the usual job descriptions (like "managed project" or "cleaned rooms"), write what the job was like in terms of your personal experience. For example, "Great money, terrible boss," or "Lots of time to myself, but paid nothing."

Now boldface the phrase *Job Qualifications*. Use bulleted points to list your best characteristics. For example:

- Loyal to my friends
- Keep my house neat
- Enjoy laughing a lot

Thinking about your jobs in terms of what they gave you, instead of what you gave your employer, might help to reveal some patterns in the type of work you prefer, or what you'd like to avoid in your next job. It also puts you in the driver's seat—you're the one who has to be pleased with your next assignment! Thinking about your best characteristics not in terms of what employers value but in terms of your whole life helps to keep your perspective on what is really important.

Ritual Specifics

Elemental energy: fire

Planetary energies: Mercury

Timing: Wednesday, any hour of Mercury or Jupiter, waxing moon/new moon

Altar cloth: red or orange

Candles: white, red, or orange

Incense: lavender or lemon

Special Tools

You can use water with a spritz of lemon juice in it as your cleansing agent. You will also need your magical resume.

Ritual Action

If you have candles, light them. For fire, light a white or red candle and say, "I invoke the power of fire." For Mercury, light a white or orange candle and say, "I invoke the power of Mercury."

Light the lavender or lemon incense from the Mercury candle. Holding the incense burner or sticks of incense in your hand, walk clockwise once around your circle, saying, "This circle fills with a vortex of energy to accomplish this rite."

Read your statement of intent, or the objective on your magical resume. Clap your hands once and say, "It is done!"

Ritual Follow-up

If you made a magical resume, mail it to yourself. If you can, mail it from a post office some distance from yours. When it returns, put it on your permanent altar or in a place where it is safe and will not be read by anyone else.

Now do the things you would normally do in a job hunt: call or write your friends and tell them you are looking for a job, read the want ads, sign up with an employment agency, mail resumes.

If you have not received a response or gotten a job interview within a reasonable amount of time (give it at least two weeks!), first examine your follow-through. Have you gotten the word out on the physical level that you're looking for a job? If you've sent out five resumes a day, phoned about ads, and had an agency interview and still have no nibbles, do a divination to ascertain what is blocking the ritual. Are you ambivalent about returning to work? Is there something you haven't paid attention to that should be in your statement of intent?

If you absolutely must have a new job immediately, are doing everything you can to find one, and your problem is just a depressed economy, you might have to change the parameters of your job search. You'd love to find a job with great hours and benefits, but for right now, you just need a paycheck! Pare down your desired result to the absolute bare necessities—for example, "I need a safe job that pays my bills." When you've adjusted your statement of intent, try ramping up the amperage of your energy with the next rite.

GET A JOB NOW!

This is an earth ritual. It can be performed on any day, in any hour, at any moon. However, it is most effective during the waxing moon, and it will harmonize with the previous rite's energy if you perform it during a Sunday or Wednesday. In this rite you will use the energy of all the elements.

Ritual Specifics
Elemental energy: earth

Timing: any day

Altar cloth: green

Candles: white or green

Incense: pine

Special Tools
Decorate the altar with money, a copy of your social security card, and the want ads from the newspaper. Have on the altar a dish of dirt, a bowl of water, and a hand fan.

Perform the Rite

Read your statement of intent.

Pick up the dirt and sprinkle it around the space. Say, "By the powers of earth, this job manifests now!" Pick up the bowl and sprinkle water around the space. Say, "By the powers of water, this job manifests now!" Light the incense and wave it around the space. Say, "By the powers of fire, this job manifests now!" Pick up the fan and wave it around the space. Say, "By the powers of air, this job manifests now!" Throw your arms out and say powerfully, "By all the powers of the elements, this job manifests *now!*"

Ritual Follow-up

When you've been employed for a while in your emergency job, come back to the job ritual and work toward upgrading your position to the job of your dreams.

Support of Your Colleagues

You got the job of your dreams. Now you need the support of the people around you to help you learn the ropes. The attitude of the people around you can make or break your experience of your job, filling the workplace with misery, or making work a happy and fun place to be.

Desired Result

What kind of relationship do you prefer to have with your coworkers? Do you want strictly professional support with little chitchat? Do you prefer a warm, family atmosphere? Do you need your manager to approve training or a vacation? Are you hoping for a birthday party at work? See if you can condense this into a single sentence, such as:

> "My colleagues provide me with mentoring
> for my professional development."

> "My management approves the training I require."

> "My coworkers are friendly and cheerful
> and we like each other a lot."

> "Our office parties are the best."

Ritual Specifics

Elemental energy: water

Planetary energy: Jupiter

Timing: Thursday, hour of Jupiter, waxing moon

Altar cloth: blue

Candles: white or blue

Incense: cedar or sage

Special Tools

If you have a photo of your coworkers, you can put that on your altar for the law of similarity. Any object with the company logo on it will also work.

Ritual Action

If you have candles, light them. For water, light a white or blue candle and say, "I invoke the power of water." For Jupiter, light a white or blue candle and say, "I invoke the power of Jupiter."

Light the cedar or sage incense from the Jupiter candle. You can also place a drop of cedar or sage oil into a bowl of water to combine the powers of Jupiter and water in this rite. You can hold the incense burner or sticks of incense in your hand, or you can hold the bowl of water and fan across it to fill the space with the scent. Walk clockwise once around your circle, saying, "This circle fills with a vortex of energy to accomplish this rite."

Read your statement of intent. Go into innerspace and imagine your colleagues surrounding you with warm smiles on their faces. Imagine what you will look and feel like when they give you the support you require.

Ritual Follow-up

If you've done a working for a specific purpose, like vacation approval, follow through by requesting the vacation. Also, remember to treat your coworkers the way you wish to be treated! If you need a mentor, find others who can use your knowledge. If you like people to be friendly, smile at them, find out their birthday dates and post them on a calendar, or leave out a dish of candy for people who visit your work area. Very shortly you will gain a reputation as a helpful or friendly person, which automatically makes people more inclined to give you what you need in return. Remember that you get back what you give out!

Need Money Now!

Something has come up: the car broke down, you had a trip to the emergency room, there's a great concert you're dying to see. What you need is an immediate burst of cash to cover the expense.

Desired Result

In this case it should be easy to write your statement of intent: "Immediate money to cover my expense!"

Ritual Specifics

Elemental energy: water

Planetary energy: Mercury

Timing: any time

Altar cloth: blue or orange

Candles: white, blue, or orange

Incense: lavender or lemon

Special Tools

Decorate the altar with your checkbook, your bank statement, and money—the biggest denomination you have, along with lots of small bills for the look and feel of prosperity.

Ritual Action

If you have candles, light them. For water, light a white or blue candle and say, "I invoke the power of water." For Mercury, light a white or orange candle and say, "I invoke the power of Mercury."

Light the lavender or lemon incense from the Mercury candle. Holding the incense burner or sticks of incense in your hand, walk clockwise once around your circle, saying, "This circle fills with a vortex of energy to accomplish this rite."

Read your statement of intent. Go into innerspace and imagine how you will look and feel when the funds arrive.

Ritual Follow-up

Walk away from this ritual and don't think about it. Act as if it has worked.

This is the kind of ritual you should only use once in a great while. If you find yourself using it more than once or twice a year, you probably need to make prosperity your magical focus for a while.

Prosperity

It's hard to focus on your spiritual enlightenment when you're worried about paying the bills or having enough to eat. The first and best use of magic is to help us lead happy, carefree lives.

Desired Result

What is prosperity? Does it mean having a lot of money? Or a lot of time? Does it mean having more than enough of everything, or just enough to live on?

Everyone has a different definition of prosperity. For me, it means having enough money to take care of my physical needs, enough money to have some fun, and still have enough time to do my personal magical work.

It can take some time to get your life to the place where you want it to be. Rituals with results like getting a job, getting a house, or arranging an emergency influx of money are rituals that need to work immediately, and it's easy to tell if they've succeeded. Other rituals are meant to be done repeatedly over long periods of time, and take longer periods of time to manifest.

One way to think about prosperity is to imagine yourself five years from now. Where will you be, what will you be wearing, and where will you be living? Imagine yourself walking through your perfect day. Try to condense this day into a single sentence. For example, "In my perfect day five years from now I live in my own house, with my best friend and lover, I own my own business, and I plan my vacation to Europe."

Also figure out a short-term goal. What do you want more of in your life right now? Do you just need more money? Would you like to have more time to yourself? Do you want a place to write or paint, or do your creative work? Would you like equipment for a hobby? Would you be happier with new furniture for your room, or a new kitchen for your house? Condense this into a single sentence too.

Make yourself a wheel of fortune for short-term prosperity. Draw a circle on a piece of paper and divide it into sections. In each section draw a picture, paste one you've cut from a magazine, or write a very short phrase describing your prosperity goal. For example, you can write the words "Great 401k," paste a picture of a new couch, or paste an ad for a trip to Europe. At the top of the page write a date, such as three months from now.

Ritual Specifics

Elemental energy: earth

Planetary energy: Jupiter

Timing: Thursday, any hour of Jupiter, waxing moon/full moon

Altar cloth: green or blue

Candles: white, green, or blue

Incense: pine, cedar

Special Tools

On your altar place your wheel of fortune and your two statements of intent. Choose a single pillar candle in a color you associate with prosperity, preferably green, white, or blue. Scratch PROSPERITY into the candle with an old ballpoint pen.

Ritual Action

If you have candles, light them. For earth, light a white or green candle and say, "I invoke the power of earth." For Jupiter, light a white or blue candle and say, "I invoke the power of Jupiter."

Light the pine incense from the earth candle. Light the cedar incense from the Jupiter candle. Holding the incense burner or sticks of incense in your hand, walk clockwise once around your circle, saying, "This circle fills with a vortex of energy to accomplish this rite."

Light the prosperity candle. Read out loud your immediate statement of intent and your long-term statement of intent. Look at the wheel of fortune and say, "My fortune manifests now!"

Ritual Follow-up

Place the prosperity candle on your permanent altar. Light it often, say every Thursday. You can repeat your statement(s) of intent or just say, "Prosperity fills my life."

Place your wheel of fortune on your permanent altar as well. You can pin it to the wall if you like. It's best to keep it in a place where only you can see it to preserve the secrecy of the ritual and keep the energy of the rite focused on the result you want. As each of the items on your wheel of fortune manifests, circle it and write above it the date that you got the item. When you've used up that wheel and everything has come into your life, make another one!

Take a Trip

You've got to get away! You need to take a vacation from your everyday life, get out of your rut, have an adventure somewhere new. Time to break out the travel magic!

I take a lot of trips, for business and for enjoyment. Vacations can be lengthy and elaborate, or quick one-day getaways. You can stay at a five-star hotel, or camp under the stars. Trips are great ways to hone your magic-making skills. When you're on the road, it becomes easier to dream about new ways to live your life, and making a little magic can pay off in big dividends.

Desired Result

Start with a simple trip close to home. Pick a place close to home that you've been meaning to go see. Is there a park, a campground, or a cute village you want to visit?

Do you plan to go by yourself, or take a friend, your spouse, or the entire family? Camping is an economical way to get out of town with a large group. You can book yourself into an inexpensive motel. If you feel like splurging, you can reserve a suite at a five-star hotel downtown and spend a night on the town! Get a photo of the place you mean to go to, or write it on a piece of paper.

Write a single sentence that describes this trip. For example:

> "I take the family to Sol Duc
> campground for the weekend."

> "My spouse and I go to
> Olympia and stay at the Motel Six."

> "I spend Saturday night at the
> Four Seasons and see an opera."

Ritual Specifics

Elemental energy: air

Planetary energy: Mercury

Timing: Wednesday, waxing/new moon

Altar cloth: yellow or orange

Candles: white, yellow, or orange

Incense: lavender or lemon

Special Tools

You will need the photo of your destination, or the paper on which you've written your destination. This activates the law of similarity.

Ritual Action

If you have candles, light them. For air, light a white or yellow candle and say, "I invoke the power of air." For Mercury, light a white or orange candle and say, "I invoke the power of Mercury."

Light the lavender or lemon incense from the Mercury candle. You can hold the incense burner or sticks of incense in your hand. You can also use a fan to fan the incense, combining the power of air with the power of Mercury. Walk clockwise once around your circle, saying, "This circle fills with a vortex of energy to accomplish this rite."

Read your statement of intent. Sit, close your eyes, and go into innerspace. Imagine yourself taking the trip.

Ritual Follow-up

Put the photo or the paper with the name of the destination on your permanent altar.

As soon as you finish the ritual, set the date for your trip. You may need to negotiate the time if you're taking others with you. If you have a job, you'll also need to request the time off. If you're staying at a hotel or a popular campground, make the reservation.

Not sure how you're going to pay for the trip? If you can't find the money in your budget anywhere, do the Need Money Now! ritual for this specific purpose.

While you're on the trip, take photos, or buy a postcard of the destination. You can put this on the wall near your permanent altar to remind yourself of the fun that you had and that you have been successful at making magic to take a trip.

Go on a Journey

Now that you've taken a small trip, it's time to work on having an adventure.

Desired Result

This is a really great chance to dream a little. If you could go anywhere in the world, where would you go? India? China? Is there one place that pops into your mind ("Oh, I've always wanted to go to . . .")? Find an image of that place: a photo for your computer, a postcard, or a magazine picture. Put that image where you can see it every day.

Get a guidebook about the place you wish to visit. The book will cover topics like types of food to eat, how to get around, the local type of money, and phrases for "hello" and "thank you." Reading about the place makes the idea of going a lot more real. Imagine yourself walking down the street, saying hello to a shopkeeper, with a pocket full of local currency. What are you wearing?

Write a single sentence that describes this journey. For example:

"I go to Nepal and drink yak butter tea
at a village teahouse."

"I go to Paris and inhale the scent of the gardens."

"I go to Rio and dance at Carnival."

You can dedicate a single yellow or orange candle to your journey. Scratch the name of the destination into it with the tip of an old ballpoint pen.

Ritual Specifics

Elemental energy: air

Planetary energy: Mercury

Timing: Wednesday, any hour of Mercury, waxing/new moon

Altar cloth: yellow or orange

Candles: white, yellow, or orange

Incense: lavender, sandalwood

Special Tools

Decorate the altar with the guidebook and photos you have collected for your journey. Set on the altar the candle that you have dedicated to your journey.

Ritual Action

If you have candles, light them. For air, light a white or yellow candle and say, "I invoke the power of air." For

Mercury, light a white or orange candle and say, "I invoke the power of Mercury."

Light the lavender or lemon incense from the Mercury candle. You can hold the incense burner or sticks of incense in your hand. You can also use a fan to fan the incense, combining the power of air with the power of Mercury. Walk clockwise once around your circle, saying, "This circle fills with a vortex of energy to accomplish this rite."

Light your journey candle and read your statement of intent.

Ritual Follow-up

Put the photo of your desired destination on your permanent altar, above the journey candle. Light the candle periodically and repeat your statement of intent.

Go to a money changer and buy a small amount of the currency of the country you plan to visit. You can put this on your altar also. If you plan to go to a country where the native tongue is not yours, buy a language tape and teach yourself a few phrases. Find a local restaurant that serves the cuisine of the country and have dinner there one night, or get a cookbook and make one of the regional specialties. Find a CD that features music of the country, or find a video about that country. Your library may have both. Have a "Journey Night" where you make yourself the country's food, play the country's music, and watch the video.

Now schedule the trip and figure out your budget. You'll need more lead time to prepare for this journey; you'll want to notify your employer a few months in advance. This will also give you time to save money. You can research budget savers, finding inexpensive lodgings and low-cost airfares. The Internet is especially good for this. You might need to do the Prosperity ritual to bring in extra money for the trip.

Write in your journal about the trip. What do you hope to get from this trip? A renewed spirit, an adventure, or a spiritual insight?

When you take the trip, gather a few mementos, things that remind you of the place where you have been. You can put these around your permanent altar, or around the house or your office, to remind yourself that you can go wherever you want to if you concentrate your magic on it!

CIRCLE OF FRIENDS

You find yourself isolated with few friends. You've just moved to a new city, or left school and found your school friends scattered, or you've focused on your job and neglected your social life. Maybe you just want to expand your circle of friends.

Being surrounded by supportive friends is one of the most important forms of wealth. Friends can support you emotionally. If you find yourself ill, friends will visit you in the hospital. True friends help you through the bad times, but all the money in the world won't help you buy friends.

I used to live in a group house with three other adults. All the people in my house were healthy, happy, and had good jobs. When we had a house fire, though, we lost most of our possessions and our place to live in a flash. This is when I found out who my true friends were. My best friend drove her car to collect us from the street where we stood in our PJs. Several friends gave us a place to stay for a few weeks while we looked for a new home. Thirty people showed up the next day to help us move out the things that hadn't been destroyed. Friends are the true gold of life.

Desired Result

Do you want to try to make one special friend, or do you want to become a member of a group of friends? Are you looking for a fairly casual relationship, like someone to go to movies and the occasional lunch with, or do you want to form a deep committed bond? Write a sentence that describes this. For example:

> "I have a best friend who knows all about me,
> supports me, and spends lots of time with me."

> "I belong to a group of friends that
> goes out together and has a good time."

> "I have a small group of friends who observe
> each other's birthdays, trade presents at Christmas,
> and are as close to each other as family."

Ritual Specifics

Elemental energy: air

Planetary energy: Venus

Timing: Friday, any hour of Venus, waxing moon

Altar cloth: yellow or green

Candles: white, yellow, or green

Incense: rose or musk

Special Tools

You will need any photo of people together laughing or hugging, or pictures of people dancing together and holding hands.

Ritual Action

If you have candles, light them. For air, light a white or yellow candle and say, "I invoke the power of air." For Venus, light a white or green candle and say, "I invoke the power of Venus."

Light the rose or musk incense from the Venus candle. You can hold the incense burner or sticks of incense in your hand. You can also use a fan to fan the incense, combining the power of air with the power of Venus. Walk clockwise once around your circle, saying, "This circle fills with a vortex of energy to accomplish this rite."

Read your statement of intent. Go into your innerspace and see yourself surrounded by caring companions. Feel the happiness and security of knowing that you have good friends.

Ritual Follow-up

If you want new people in your life, you need to get yourself into a place where you can find them. Take a class in something that interests you, or join a club. Talk to the people there. If you find yourself having a lot of conversations with a particular person, ask him or her out to lunch or dinner.

Since you're a magician, you might consider joining a magical club or group. Magicians are often receptive to the idea of families of friends. Some organizations take the bonds of fraternity very seriously and you will find supportive relationships there. Members of Wiccan covens often consider themselves closer than blood relatives.

As with the circle of colleagues, you will get back what you put out. Be friendly to others, and they will be more inclined to be friendly to you! Ask your new friends how they feel, and really listen to the response. Tell them what is going on in your life too; don't hide yourself, waiting for them to ask.

Friendship is an intangible. It means more than just getting back what you give out, or making sure you're taken care of. It is valuable in and of itself in ways that are impossible to measure. It is a bond between people that makes life richer and more interesting. Having friends is one of the joys of being alive.

Control Time

Do you need more time in your day? Can't find a free weekend to take the trip you want to take? Are you enjoying your job but working a lot of overtime and need a chance to relax? Did you have all your activities set for the month and now everyone wants to change their mind? You need to take control of your time.

Desired Result

Saturn is the power to call on. This planet, called Cronos (which means "time") by the Greeks, governs all things having to do with your schedule. Be careful with this power though. Saturn tends to solidify things, so if what you want is more freedom, it will pay to spend some time wording your desired result. Here are some examples:

> "I find enough time in my schedule
> to go to the gym three times this week."

> "Next month I have a free weekend to take my trip."

> "The overtime lets up on me this week
> so I can spend time with my family."

"My schedule firms up and everyone
keeps their commitments."

Make a copy of a calendar page, or use a scheduling software program. Write on it the events you wish to have happen. You can write the specific event, like "Vacation to Tahiti," or you can write "My time!"

Ritual Specifics

Elemental energy: earth

Planetary energy: Saturn

Timing: Saturday, any hour of Saturn, waning moon

Altar cloth: green or black

Candles: white, green or black

Incense: pine, and myrrh or civet

Special Tool

Place your calendar on the altar.

Ritual Action

If you have candles, light them. For earth, light a white or green candle and say, "I invoke the power of earth." For Saturn, light a white or black candle and say, "I invoke the power of Saturn."

Light the pine incense from the earth candle. Light the myrrh or civet incense from the Saturn candle. Walk clockwise once around your circle, saying, "This circle fills with a vortex of energy to accomplish this rite."

Read your schedule out loud. Tap it once and say, "My time is mine!"

Ritual Follow-up

Put the calendar in your notebook. When you get your time off, be sure to go back and note this on the calendar.

For Justice

There are many times in life that call for an appeal for justice. A burglar broke into your house, or someone hit your car and sped off. You were passed over for promotion, again, because of your sex or your race. An ex-friend took advantage of you, borrowed something, and didn't return it. Someone is telling stories about you. Whatever the situation, you feel aggrieved, and that feeling is getting in the way of all your other magic. You need to ground out your emotion, all your fear and anger, and put yourself back in a position of power again.

Desired Result

To work this rite, write out your grievance. Talk about exactly what happened to you. Don't hold back; put all of your emotion into it, and as much detail as you can. For example, "I loaned my friend my car, and when he returned it, its front end was completely scrunched. I feel so stupid for letting him drive it! I'm so angry with him for hurting my car." Stick to talking about what happened, and how you feel about it.

Ritual Specifics

Elemental energy: air

Planetary energy: Saturn

Timing: Saturday, any hour of Saturn, waning moon

Altar cloth: yellow or black

Candles: white, yellow, or black

Incense: myrrh, civet

Special Tools

Bring your written grievance and a black feather.

Ritual Action

If you have candles, light them. For air, light a white or yellow candle and say, "I invoke the power of air." For Saturn, light a white or black candle and say, "I invoke the power of Saturn."

Light the myrrh or civet incense from the Saturn candle. You can hold the incense burner or sticks of incense in your hand. You can also use a fan to fan the incense, combining the power of air with the power of Saturn. Walk clockwise once around your circle, saying, "This circle fills with a vortex of energy to accomplish this rite."

Now sit, take a deep breath, and calmly read your grievance. When you have finished, fold it up and put it on your altar. Tap it and say, "All that was taken from me returns to me." If you have a black feather, blow across it. Say, "This matter is brought to justice."

Ritual Follow-up

Take the grievance and bury it.

Now is the time to turn your thoughts away from the matter. You've given justice over to the powers of Saturn, who will take care of it for you. Fretting about it will hinder the rite.

This is an excellent ritual to perform along with the ritual for emotional healing and the rite for protection. You can combine them all into one ritual. Don't worry about the elemental or planetary attributions, just cleanse and consecrate the jewelry.

Remember that justice is not revenge. In the heat of anger it may be difficult to tell the difference. The magic of justice restores to you what was unjustly taken from you. It does not punish the person who hurt you. The focus of this ritual is not to cause pain to someone else but specifically to protect and heal you. Revenge is a form of magic, but it is volatile and exacts significant cost, and for those reasons there is no revenge ritual in this book.

EMOTIONAL HEALING

Something hurts; you lost something, or someone. We all sustain losses in life, and what seems like a minor problem to others might hit really hard. It's time to pay attention to healing.

Desired Result

The most important thing is to acknowledge that it hurts, and that it's okay to hurt. Spend some time with your grief. Live through it. Talk about it with your friends, cry, and/or write in your journal.

You might not be dealing with a major trauma, but you've had a really bad week: the boss yelled at you, you fought with a friend, you dinged the car, bounced a check, and the whole thing has left you frazzled and tense.

Think about the peace and happiness you would like to experience again. Put this in a single sentence. For example:

"My heart lifts and I can smile again."

"I am relaxed and calm."

Ritual Specifics

Elemental energy: water

Planetary energy: moon

Timing: Monday, any hour of the moon, waning moon

Altar cloth: blue, white, or silver

Candles: white, blue, or silver

Incense: jasmine, gardenia

Special Tools

You will need a bowl of water. You can place a drop of jasmine or gardenia oil in the water. Also bring a piece of jewelry that represents you, like a ring or necklace you often wear.

Ritual Action

If you have candles, light them. For water, light a white or blue candle and say, "I invoke the power of water." For the moon, light a white or silver candle and say, "I invoke the power of the moon."

Light the jasmine or gardenia incense from the moon candle. You can hold the incense burner or sticks of incense in your hand. Walk clockwise once around your circle, saying, "This circle fills with a vortex of energy to accomplish this rite."

Read your statement of intent. Next, take the jewelry that represents you. Dip it into the water and say, "I am washed clean. I am healed and renewed."

Ritual Follow-up

You can follow up with a bath of your own. Place the moon and water candles at the rim of the tub to bring their power into your bath. Wrap yourself in something warm and spend an evening taking care of yourself: drink warm milk, read a soothing story, listen to soft music. Remember to take it easy on yourself for a few days as you recover your emotional poise.

PROTECTION

You feel threatened; something seems to menace you. Maybe you just feel it's time to pay attention to your safety. Your next ritual act is to do a rite of protection.

Desired Result

You can perform this rite for yourself. You can also perform this ritual for someone else. You should definitely talk to and obtain permission from that person before you send him or her energy. Otherwise you can disorient the person, and he or she won't necessarily know what to do with the energy. This is polite magical behavior. The exception to this rule is when you are doing the ritual on behalf of your own children or pets, beings for whom you have responsibility. Even then it's a good idea to talk to them (yes, talk to your pet) and explain what you are doing and why.

Describe your desire for safety in a single sentence. For example:

"I am protected at home, at
work, at school, and on the street."

"My daughter is protected wherever she goes."

"I am safe and happy in my life."

Ritual Specifics

Elemental energy: fire

Planetary energy: Mars

Timing: Tuesday, any hour of Mars, waxing moon

Altar cloth: red

Candles: white or red

Incense: cinnamon (or a spicy scent)

Special Tools

You will need a bowl of water. You can add a drop of cinnamon or pennyroyal oil to the water. Also bring a protective amulet, such as a ring or necklace, a pin, or a semiprecious stone to carry in your pocket.

Ritual Action

If you have candles, light them. For fire, light a white or red candle and say, "I invoke the power of fire." For Mars, light a white or red candle and say, "I invoke the power of Mars."

Light the cinnamon incense from the Mars candle. You can hold the incense burner or sticks of incense in your hand. Walk clockwise once around your circle, saying, "This circle fills with a vortex of energy to accomplish this rite."

Read your statement of intent. Dip the amulet into the water and say, "This amulet is cleansed of all energies except that of my purpose." Wave the amulet through the incense and say, "This amulet is charged to protect [*name of the person to be protected*]."

Ritual Follow-up

If the amulet is for you, put it on. If it is for someone else, give it to that person.

If you are threatened by a specific person, take the appropriate steps to guard yourself against that person. This is also a good time to review your house security system and check the locks on the doors and windows. This is also a good time to renew the wards on your house and car.

Physical Healing

Our physical bodies sustain a lot of damage in the course of a lifetime. There are minor wounds, such as sprained muscles, cuts, and burns. Some injuries are immediate and more serious, like broken bones or a virus that infects us. Most seriously, we can contract a long-term illness, like cancer.

Of course the first thing to do when you sustain a physical injury is to see a doctor! Magic is not a substitute for professional medical care. Magic aids and augments what the healing profession will do for you. Also, assist in your own recovery by researching, reading, and talking to others with your ailment, so that you have as much knowledge as you can. Then, when you have done all the things you need to do on the physical level, you can bring that information to bear in creating your healing ritual.

Desired Result

Write the nature of your illness on a small piece of paper. For example, "Broken arm bone," "Walking pneumonia," or "Cancer of the skin."

Next, summarize your desired healthy state in a single sentence. For example:

"I pitch at my office softball game."

"I am energetic and whole."

"My skin is clear and smooth again."

Ritual Specifics

Elemental energy: earth

Planetary energy: Mercury

Timing: Wednesday, any hour of Mercury, waning moon

Altar cloth: green or orange

Candles: white, green, or orange

Incense: pine, and lavender or lemon

Special Tools

You will need your illness description and a fireproof container, like an ashtray, an iron pot, or a dish of sand. Also bring a cup of healing tea, like comfrey or mint.

Ritual Action

If you have candles, light them. For earth, light a white or green candle and say, "I invoke the power of earth." For Mercury, light a white or orange candle and say, "I invoke the power of Mercury."

Light the pine incense from the earth candle. Light the lavender or lemon incense from the Mercury candle. You can hold the incense burner or sticks of incense in your hand. Walk clockwise once around your circle, saying, "This circle fills with a vortex of energy to accomplish this rite."

Read your statement of intent. Take the paper on which you have written your illness and burn it. Say, "This illness passes out of my life." Take a deep breath and exhale, feeling and seeing the illness flow out of your body.

Now hold the cup of tea in your hands. Inhale its aroma, feeling and seeing it fill your body with healthy energy. Drink it slowly. Say, "I am whole and healthy again."

Ritual Follow-up

Be sure to take the ashes of the paper and dispose of them outside. Toss them into running water, or bury them in the earth.

Follow through with the things you need to do to heal, such as see the doctor, take your medicine, or stay in bed. The ritual brings magic to bear to help you heal faster, but your body has to do the work!

HEALING ANOTHER

Someone you care about is ill and you'd like to help him or her.

Desired Result

First, ask the person in need if he or she would welcome your magical help! If you send energy to people who aren't expecting it and who may not welcome it, you can do more harm than good.

Once you've received permission for your healing work, ask the person to define his or her ailment in a single sentence. Write it on a small piece of paper.

Ritual Specifics

Elemental energy: earth

Planetary energy: Mercury

Timing: Wednesday, any hour of Mercury, waning moon

Altar cloth: green or orange

Candles: white, green, or orange

Incense: pine, and lavender or lemon

Special Tools

You will need something that represents your friend: a photo, an object he or she owns, his or her name on a piece of paper. Also bring the paper with the illness description; a fireproof container, like an ashtray, an iron pot, or a dish of sand; and a cup of healing tea, like comfrey or mint.

Ritual Action

If you have candles, light them. For earth, light a white or green candle and say, "I invoke the power of earth." For Mercury, light a white or orange candle and say, "I invoke the power of Mercury."

Light the pine incense from the earth candle. Light the lavender or lemon incense from the Mercury candle. You can hold the incense burner or sticks of incense in your hand. Walk clockwise once around your circle, saying, "This circle fills with a vortex of energy to accomplish this rite."

Read your statement of intent. Take the paper on which you have written the illness description and burn it. Say, "This illness leaves [*your friend's name*]." Visualize your friend, and feel and see the illness flowing away.

Now place the cup of tea in front of the object representing your friend. Feel and see healthy energy infusing your friend. Say, "[*Your friend's name*] is whole and healthy again."

Ritual Follow-up

Keep track of your friend's progress. You can follow this up with a get-well present. If your friend welcomes magic, you can give him or her the candle that you used in this rite. Tell your friend to light the candle for a few minutes every day (making sure to watch while it burns!) until he or she is well.

A New Love

You are finally at a place in your life where you can think about love. You've grown up, recovered from a breakup, or your career has stabilized and you have some free time. You're tired of being alone. It's time to invite love into your life!

Desired Result

What do you want from a lover? Are you looking for your one true love that will last forever? Are you pining for a summer fling before you go to school? If you're polyamorous, how about about an additional lover to add to an already happy love life? Here are a few things to think about:

- How much time do you have to spend on a relationship?

- Are you looking for a part-time relationship, or do you have lots of space in your life for someone to fill?

- What's important to you in a relationship?

- Do you want lots of hot sex, just a little, or none at all?

- Do you long for someone to share your passions and dreams, or do you just want someone to go to movies with now and again?

- Must your new partner share your religion, your age, race, and/or the city in which you live?

Distill your requirements into a single sentence. For example:

> "I find my soul mate and we
> travel the world studying art."

> "An easy, gentle romance comes into my life."

> "I find an uncomplicated relationship
> with lots of sex and good times."

Don't be afraid to ask for what you want! You don't have to justify it to your family or friends. This is just for you—you're putting it out in ritual for the universe to manifest.

Ritual Specifics

Elemental energy: fire

Planetary energy: Venus

Timing: Friday, any hour of Venus, waxing moon, especially new moon

Altar cloth: red or green

Candles: white, red, or green

Incense: rose or musk

Special Tools

You will need your statement of intent. Also bring a candle to represent your new love: white, pink (especially for light romances), red, or any color that you feel represents your desires.

Ritual Action

If you have candles, light them. For fire, light a white or red candle and say, "I invoke the power of fire." For Venus, light a white or green candle and say, "I invoke the power of Venus."

Light the rose or musk incense from the Venus candle. You can hold the incense burner or sticks of incense in your hand. Walk clockwise once around your circle, saying, "This circle fills with a vortex of energy to accomplish this rite."

Read your statement of intent. Light the candle that represents your new love. Say, "Like sun and moon, like day and night, like spring and fall, I call my love to me." This activates the process of polarity.

Ritual Follow-up

Put the candle on your permanent altar. Every Friday, light it and repeat the polarity invocation ("Like sun and moon...").

One good way to think about attracting a lover is to think about attracting a friend. You can combine this ritual with the Circle of Friends rite. If you don't like the whole process of dating, you can try to make new friends and see if one of those friendships leads to romance.

You can also place a personal ad. Use the ad you intend to place as your statement of intent.

Sustain a Love

You and your lover have been together for some time. There have been a lot of wonderful times, some fights and sadnesses too, but mostly you remember the laughter and joy. Now you're moving out of that first blush of excitement. You're making the transition to figuring out how the two of you are going to love each other over the long haul. It can be a little frightening to feel that initial rush of passion fade out. You want to hang on to it, and you worry that your lover may end your relationship to find the excitement of first passion again with someone new.

Desired Result

The first thing to decide is if you really want this person in your life more permanently. Is it better to let him or her fade away? Maybe with the passion over, you can become permanent ex-lovers and friends. If you feel more relief than sadness when you think about this, you might consider this option.

If you strongly react against that thought and you truly want a deep, long-lasting romance with this person (maybe even a long-term commitment or marriage), then this ritual is for you.

Think about the form you want your relationship to take. Now that you know your lover, you know what your strengths are together, and you also know your weaknesses. Write a statement of intent that accentuates your strengths and balances out the places where you need to do some work.

Say you have lots of fun together, but you sometimes fight bitterly. You want a long-term romance. Your statement of intent might say, "My lover and I stick together, we learn how to resolve our conflicts calmly, and we have more and more fun with each other."

Ritual Specifics

Elemental energy: water

Planetary energy: sun

Timing: Sunday, any hour of the sun, waxing moon, especially full moon

Altar cloth: blue or yellow

Candles: white, red, or yellow

Incense: frankincense or sandalwood

Special Tools

You will need a gift your lover has given you. You can also buy a gift for your lover.

Ritual Action

If you have candles, light them. For water, light a white or blue candle and say, "I invoke the power of water." For the sun, light a white or yellow candle and say, "I invoke the power of the sun."

Light the frankincense or sandalwood incense from the sun candle. You can hold the incense burner or sticks of incense in your hand. Walk clockwise once around your circle, saying, "This circle fills with a vortex of energy to accomplish this rite."

Read your statement of intent. Hold the gift your lover gave you and say, "As my love gave this gift to me, so my love gives me the gift of enduring love." Hold the gift you mean to give your lover and say, "As I give this gift to my lover, so I give my lover the gift of my enduring love."

Ritual Follow-up

Give the gift to your lover. Put the gift your lover gave you in a place where you can see it every day. If it's jewelry, wear it.

The most important thing to do next is to talk to your lover! You can't build the relationship you want by yourself. Let your lover know exactly what you want. Talk about the ways you think you can overcome the rough spots in your relationship, and especially talk about what you love about that person, and how much you want to go on loving.

Release a Love

It's time to let your lover go. You're fighting more than you're having fun. It's become clear to you that this person has a negative impact on your life. What seemed like support turns out to be a need to control, or what seemed like charming honesty turns out to be rudeness. It could be that it's gotten really ugly, and you're hurting a lot. It's time to end this relationship and move on with your life.

Desired Result

Deciding to end a relationship is one of the toughest choices you can ever make. You're bound to have a lot of feelings, such as anger, sorrow, or frustration. Maybe you weren't the person who decided to end the relationship. Even so, it's clear that it's over, and you feel the need to ritually sever your ties with this person and move on.

Confront your anger; get it out of your system. Write down all the things that made you unhappy, and the reasons why you are ending this relationship.

Confront your sorrow. Write down the things that you liked about the relationship that you're going to miss.

Finally, write the outcome that you want. Do you want to remain friends with this person? Do you want to never see or speak to him or her again? Remember to add that you want to be at peace, and to be free to love again.

Ritual Specifics

Elemental energy: water

Planetary energy: Mars

Timing: Tuesday, any hour of Mars, waning moon, especially dark moon

Altar cloth: blue or red

Candles: white, blue, or red

Incense: cinnamon or any spicy scent

Special Tools

Besides the incense listed above, you will need a stick of incense—it has to be a stick. This incense will remain unlit. Also bring a photo of your lover, your descriptions of your anger and sorrow, and your statement of intent.

Ritual Action

If you have candles, light them. For water, light a white or blue candle and say, "I invoke the power of water." For Mars, light a white or red candle and say, "I invoke the power of the Mars."

Light the cinnamon or spice incense from the Mars candle. You can hold the incense burner or sticks of incense in your hand. Walk clockwise once around your circle, saying, "This circle fills with a vortex of energy to accomplish this rite."

Read your statement of intent. Sit in front of your altar and look at the photo of your lover. Read the pages you wrote about your anger and your sorrow to that person. Now take the stick of incense, say, "We two are parted," and break it in half. Turn the photo over.

Ritual Follow-up

Again, communicate your desired outcome to your ex-lover. Let your ex know that it's over, that you want to stay friends, that you never want to see that person again, or whatever you choose to do.

You may choose to share your letters of anger and sorrow with your ex. If you want to remain friends, however, it's probably a good idea to simply file them in your magical notebook.

You might follow up this ritual with the ritual for emotional healing. Now is also a good time to focus on any other magic at all—take a trip, work on your career, expand your circle of friends. You will know when you are ready for a new love again.

CREATIVE INSPIRATION

You are an artist, writer, or musician ready to start a new project. You make handcrafts and want to be more expressive with your craft. Maybe you'd like to explore a creative side and you're not really sure what form it will take. You need inspiration!

Desired Result

Do you want to start a new project or finish an existing one? Do you just want to invite increased creativity into your life? Write your desire in a single sentence. Here are some examples:

"I am inspired to finish the book I am writing."

"I get lots of new ideas for my new paintings."

"Creativity comes into my life
in many pleasant new ways."

Ritual Specifics

Elemental energy: air

Planetary energy: moon

Timing: Monday, any hour of the moon, waxing moon,
   especially new moon

Altar cloth: yellow or silver

Candles: white, yellow, or silver

Incense: jasmine or gardenia

Special Tool
You will need a crystal.

Ritual Action
If you have candles, light them. For air, light a white or
yellow candle and say, "I invoke the power of air." For the
moon, light a white or silver candle and say, "I invoke the
power of the moon."

   Light the jasmine or gardenia incense from the moon
candle. You can hold the incense burner or sticks of
incense in your hand. Walk clockwise once around your
circle, saying, "This circle fills with a vortex of energy to
accomplish this rite."

   Read your statement of intent. If you have a crystal,
hold it in your hand and say, "This crystal fills with the
energy of creative inspiration."

Ritual Follow-up
Pay special attention to your dreams immediately after
this ritual. If you haven't made a dream journal, now is a
good time to start one. You can leave your crystal out

where it can capture the light of the moon. Sleep with it near your bed. You can also hold it or place it near you when you work on your creative projects.

Find a Spiritual Path

You feel a call, a need to understand something more about how the world works and the forces of the universe beyond yourself. The religion of your childhood doesn't seem to meet your needs any longer. You've found something about what you've been looking for in magic, but you know you want to learn more. You'd like to choose a magical path.

Desired Result

What are you seeking in a spiritual path? Do you want a religion that describes deity and the workings of the universe? Are you more interested in a philosophy with less emphasis on external rules and greater emphasis on finding yourself?

Are you looking for a group of people to share your spirituality? A single teacher who will help you figure out where you need to go? Are you most interested in exploring your spirituality on your own?

Summarize your desires in a sentence. Here are some examples:

"I find the religion that is right for me."

"I find a group of people who can spend time with me and meet together to discuss spiritual growth."

"I attract the perfect teacher who helps me understand where I need to go."

"My spiritual understanding becomes clear to me."

Ritual Specifics

Elemental energy: fire

Planetary energy: sun

Timing: Sunday, any hour of the sun, waxing moon, especially full moon

Altar cloth: red or yellow

Candles: white, red, or yellow

Incense: frankincense or sandalwood

Special Tool

You will need your statement of intent.

Ritual Action

If you have candles, light them. For fire, light a white or red candle and say, "I invoke the power of fire." For the sun, light a white or yellow candle and say, "I invoke the power of the sun."

Light the frankincense or sandalwood incense from the sun candle. You can hold the incense burner or sticks of incense in your hand. Walk clockwise once around your circle, saying, "This circle fills with a vortex of energy to accomplish this rite."

Read your statement of intent. Close your eyes and enter innerspace. See and feel what you will look and sound like when you have found your spiritual path.

Ritual Follow-up

Read books; explore classes in your area. Every metropolitan area in the world has magical and spiritual resources that are easily available if you look for them.

Just a word of caution: in the first heady rush of exploring a new way of being, it's easy to be swept away in enthusiasm. It's very much like falling in love: everything seems wonderful and new, and you are filled with happiness and a new sense of freedom. Just as in love, some of this new enthusiasm stays with you for the rest of your life, and some of it turns out to be bad for you. Also, there are people who move in during that initial excitement and use your newfound sense of freedom to take advantage of you. Think of them as spiritual pickpockets, taking advantage of you after you've had a drink and are walking on an unfamiliar street.

A simple dose of common sense can keep you out of a lot of trouble. If your new friends seem to want a lot of money from you, ask you to move, want you to give up your job, your spouse, your other friends, or basically make a huge change in your life, they're probably more interested in what they can get out of you than in helping you find your spiritual center. There are many spiritual teachers who will ask you to examine your life and make decisions based on what's right for you. You may decide that you want to change your job or move, but then it will be your decision based on your newfound sense of self, and not a decision someone else is making for you. You might pair this ritual with the ritual of protection just to make sure that you stay on the path that is best for you.

This is the most powerful ritual in this book. Of course it is important to have a place to live and a way to support yourself, to be physically and emotionally healthy, to have friends, and to have love in your life. Love is a powerful and potent force that can substantially alter everything else.

However, it is your spiritual path that most intimately dictates who you are in the world. By this I don't mean the religion you profess or who your teacher is. I mean that core of understanding of the world and yourself that guides you in your day-to-day life. When you are on the right spiritual path, tremendous energy is available to you to make everything else happen—the job, the money, the friends, and the love will all fall into place.

The clearest mark of the magician is the conscious choice of a spiritual path.

Afterword

In this book you have learned how to see and feel the magic in the world and how to bring it into your life. The exercises in each chapter build skills that are immediately useful and will remain useful for the rest of your life. The ritual outline gives you an example of a way to create ritual space. The rituals themselves cover most of the issues we face in the day-to-day world: having a place to live, having an income to live on, physical and emotional health and safety, friends, lovers, creative inspiration, and spiritual development.

These skills and rituals are all that you need in order to live a happy magical life. Some magicians go on to explore various branches of magical religion and philosophy, including Wicca, Paganism, Thelema, and ceremonial magic; Voudoun, Tantra, Huna, and many, many other disciplines and faiths. You may choose one of those magical paths, or you may choose to use magic to keep your life on the track you want to follow. There are no rules about what you must do. The choices are entirely yours.

There are just a few rules of thumb that will make your way a little easier as you continue your career in the magical world.

You are your own best teacher. You may read many books, take classes, find a teacher, or take on a lifelong commitment to a group, but whatever you do, you are always in charge of your own learning process. Only you can ultimately decide whether what you are learning is working for you. If you've given a course a serious try, and you believe you're wasting your time, move on to another course. The freedom, responsibility, and authority rests entirely with you.

Listen to yourself. The conscious mind is a small percentage of your total mental and spiritual being. Sometimes you consciously make a choice that you know on some level isn't right for you. At other times, parts of you know something that you haven't yet learned consciously. Your body will try to tell you by getting sick. Your dreams will tell you. The intuition in your belly is seldom wrong. Much of magical skill centers around learning to pay attention to the signals you are giving yourself. If something in your life seems out of whack, or you feel that something wonderful is about to happen, look to your personal signals for clues about what's going on. You already know.

Observe the world. You are embedded in a complex matrix of life. Every second of every day your senses absorb more information than you can process; you throw away most of what you see, hear, and feel because you just can't handle the load. The stuff that you filter out is what seems to be magical when it breaks through to your consciousness. The "extra-normal" senses and phenomena aren't really out of the ordinary, they're part of what makes the world work. They are just outside of our current culturally agreed-upon description of reality. If you suspend judgment and carefully watch, listen, and feel the world around you, you will discover amazing things that will expand the limits of what you thought was possible.

Life is magical. This book is one of the ways in which you can begin to tune into the magic. There are many others. It's up to you to find them.

Glossary

asana: A position of the body in yogic practice that increases physical flexibility and stimulates the body's energy.

Beltane: One of the eight holidays of Witchcraft. Held on May 1 as a celebration of spring, with a special emphasis on love and marriage.

ceremonial magic: A Western philosophical system that includes the practice of ritual for personal development.

chakra: A center of energy in the body usually located along the spine.

Chaldea: An ancient civilization that studied and named the planets.

chi: A Chinese word describing the magical energy of the body. *See also* ki.

circle: A boundary of energy enclosing a space to contain a ritual.

deosil: A clockwise movement in a ritual.

divination: Using a magical technique or tool to predict the result of a particular ritual action.

grounding energy: Putting excess energy from ritual back into the ground.

Hellenistic culture: A mixture of Greek, Roman, and Egyptian culture in the first few centuries of the common era.

Hermetica: A group of Hellenistic philosophical and religious texts.

Huna: A Hawaiian folk religion with a special emphasis on healing.

I Ching: A Chinese divination system made up of symbols called *hexagrams,* which have philosophical and practical interpretations.

ki: A Japanese word describing the magical energy of the body. *See also* chi.

kundalini: Tantric sexual energy that travels from the base of the torso up the spine to the top of the head.

mandala: A Tibetan diagram of the cosmos that includes a center and symmetrical parts arranged around the center.

medium: A person who contacts the spirits of the dead.

meridian: A column of magical energy in the body.

moontime: A woman's menstrual period.

Neopagan: A person practicing a religion that revives and continues one of the ancient European folk religions.

Neuro-Linguistic Programming: A psychology that emphasizes practical results in daily life.

one point: The body's energy center in the abdomen. *See also* tan t'ien.

polyamory: Having serious romantic relationships with more than one person at the same time.

phenomenology: A discipline that studies how humans perceive the world.

psychometry: Learning about an object by psychically reading it.

Qabalah: A Jewish religious philosophy adopted by ceremonial magicians.

Samhain: One of the eight holidays of Witchcraft. Held on October 31 as a celebration of fall, with a special emphasis on honoring the dead.

scrying: The psychic ability to forsee the future by looking into an object such as a crystal ball or dish of water.

seership: The learned ability to see energy and spirits made of energy.

spellcraft: Using magical tools and techniques to accomplish a desired result.

Sufism: A mystical Islamic sect. The members of Sufism are also known as *whirling dervishes,* and they use dance and movement as a way to feel oneness with the divine.

synthema: An ancient Greek term for objects that embody the energy of the planets.

Tantra: A religious philosophy practiced by both Buddhists and Hindus that contains techniques for directing the body's energy, especially sexual energy.

Tarot: A deck of cards that includes an additional suit called the *major arcana,* used as a form of divination.

tan t'ien: A Chinese word describing the body's energy center in the abdomen. *See also* one point.

telepathy: Two human minds sharing words, pictures, or ideas without verbally expressing them.

Thelema: A religious philosophy founded by Aleister Crowley that emphasizes personal responsibility and treasures personal liberty.

Voudoun: A Caribbean religion mixing Christianity with African folk religion.

Wicca: Also called *Witchcraft;* a religion revived in the 1900s that centers on Goddess worship and living in harmony with nature.

widdershins: A counterclockwise movement in a ritual.

yoga: An ancient movement discipline that moves energy by positioning the physical body.

Bibliography

This is a short annotated bibliography, focusing on texts that are directly related to the techniques in this book. Here are the places to explore some of these subjects more specifically and in-depth.

Andrews, Ted. *How to See and Read the Aura*. St. Paul, MN: Llewellyn Publications, 1991.

A simple technique for training yourself to see and feel the energy signature of the human body.

Berendt, Joachim-Ernst. *The Third Ear: On Listening to the World*. Shaftesbury, England: Element, 1988.

Berendt has many insights about music and sound and how they shape the world.

———. *The World Is Sound: Nada Brahma Music and the Landscape of Consciousness.* Rochester, VT: Destiny Books, 1991.

A fairly extensive treatise on the esoteric understanding of sound derived from the study of Indian classical music.

Crowley, Aleister. *777 and Other Qabalistic Writings of Aleister Crowley.* 1912. Reprint, York Beach, ME: Samuel Weiser, 1973.

The essential reference text for planetary and elemental attributions.

Dean, Liz. *The Art of Tarot.* New York: Michael Friedman Publishing Group, 2002.

An easily accessible Tarot deck illustrated by Emma Garner, along with a short interpretive book by Dean. A very good first deck.

Garfield, Patricia. *Creative Dreaming.* New York: Simon & Schuster, 1974.

One of the books that articulated modern dreamwork techniques. Particularly useful in learning to keep a dream diary.

Gawain, Shakti. *Creative Visualization.* Berkeley, CA: Whatever Publications, 1978.

One of the classic texts describing affirmation and visualization techniques and the power they unleash to direct your life.

Godwin, Joscelyn. *The Mystery of the Seven Vowels.* Grand Rapids, MI: Phanes Press, 1991.

An interesting technique equating the vowels with tones and colors. Explores the ancient as well as magical uses of these sounds.

Grinder, John, and Richard Bandler. *Frogs into Princes.* Moab, UT: Real People, 1981.

———. *ReFraming: Neuro-Linguistic Programming and the Transformation of Meaning.* Moab, UT: Real People, 1979.

———. *Trance-Formations: Neuro-Linguistic Programming and the Structure of Hypnosis.* Moab, UT: Real People, 1981.

These three books are the introductory volumes to Neuro-Linguistic Programming, taught as a type of therapy, but also as a way to learn to relate to others. *Trance-Formations* discusses ways of inducing trance, and *Reframing* teaches storytelling. Indispensable training in observation and communication.

Progoff, Ira. *At a Journal Workshop.* New York: Dialogue House, 1975.

———. *The Practice of Process Meditation.* New York: Dialogue House, 1980.

Progoff's intensive journal method is a particular form of journal-keeping that delves quite deeply into the diarist's emotions, worldview, and experiences. Good for in-depth exploration of the possibilities of the journal.

Rainier, Tristine. *The New Diary: How to Use a Journal for Self-Guidance and Expanded Creativity.* East Rutherford, NJ: Putnam Publishing Group, 1979.

Rainier covers basic journal-keeping techniques and issues, and includes discussions on integrating the journal with a dream record, the diary as therapy, and the diary as a form of conscious magic.

Roberts, Jane. *The Nature of Personal Reality.* New York: Bantam Books, 1984.

————. *Seth Speaks.* New York: Bantam Books, 1984.

Roberts was one of the earliest channelers. Unlike the Spiritualists, who talked to deceased spirits, channelers often talk to spirits of other galaxies. Roberts's contact Seth is an extraterrestrial spirit. Whatever your personal belief system, the Seth books form an interesting challenge to the way we think about how the world works.

Silva, Jose. *Silva Mind Control Method.* New York: Pocket Books, 1982.

Silva combined self-hypnosis with visualization and affirmation techniques, along with some creative therapeutic ideas of his own, to create a system that introduced many people to the idea that you can shape your own life.

Tohei, Koichi. *Ki in Daily Life.* Ki No Kenyukai, Japan: Japan Publications Trading Company, 1978.

This book outlines the basics of martial arts training, including energy exercises, breathing, and discipline.

Deceptively simple, foundational training. The most important book in this bibliography.

Waite, Arthur Edward. *The Original Rider Waite Tarot Pack.* 1909. Reprint, Stamford, CT: U.S. Games, 1993.

Illustrated by Pamela Colman Smith, this was the first deck to include pictures on the court cards. The classic first deck for many practitioners of magic.

Williams, Strephon Kaplan. *The Jungian-Senoi Dreamwork Manual.* Berkeley, CA: Journey Press, 1980.

As the Senoi have become integrated into the worldwide communication network, they have clarified their dream-work techniques, which turn out to be very different than the romantic fantasy spun by the people who initially popularized their name. That said, this book is largely based on the modern work of Williams and others who are inventing very interesting techniques for remembering, understanding, and interacting with the dreaming process.

Index

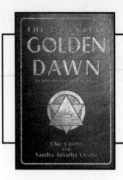

The Essential Golden Dawn

An Introduction to High Magic

CHIC CICERO AND
SANDRA TABATHA CICERO

Is the Golden Dawn system for you? Today the Golden Dawn is one of the most sought-after and respected systems of magic in the world. Over a century old, it's considered the capstone of the Western Esoteric Tradition, yet many of the available books on the subject are too complex or overwhelming for readers just beginning to explore alternative spiritual paths.

The Essential Golden Dawn is for those who simply want to find out what the Golden Dawn is and what it has to offer. It answers questions such as: What is Hermeticism? How does magic work? Who started the Golden Dawn? What are its philosophies and principles? It helps readers determine whether this system is for them, and then it guides them into further exploration as well as basic ritual work.

0-7387-0310-9
360 pp., 6 x 9 $16.95

How to See and Read the Aura

TED ANDREWS

Everyone has an aura—the three-dimensional, shape-and-color-changing energy field that surrounds all matter—and anyone can learn to see and experience the aura more effectively. There is nothing magical about the process. It simply involves a little understanding, time, practice, and perseverance.

Do some people make you feel drained? Do you find some rooms more comfortable and enjoyable to be in? Have you ever been able to sense the presence of other people before you actually heard or saw them? If so, you have experienced another person's aura. In this practical, easy-to-read manual, you receive a variety of exercises to practice alone and with partners to build your skills in aura reading and interpretation. Also, you will learn to balance your aura each day to keep it vibrant and strong so others cannot drain your vital force.

Learning to see the aura not only breaks down old barriers—it also increases sensitivity. As we develop the ability to see and feel the more subtle aspects of life, our intuition unfolds and increases, and the childlike joy and wonder of life returns.

0-87542-013-3

160 pp., 4³⁄₁₆ x 6⅞, illus. $5.99

Practical Guide to Psychic Self-Defense
Strengthen Your Aura
DENNING & PHILLIPS

Psychic well-being and psychic self-defense are two sides of the same coin, just as are physical health and resistance to disease. Each person (and every living thing) is surrounded by an electromagnetic force field, or aura, that can provide the means to psychic self-defense and to dynamic well-being. This book explores the world of very real "psychic warfare" of which we are all victims.

Every person in our modern world is subjected to psychic stress and psychological bombardment: advertising promotions that play upon primitive emotions, political and religious appeals that work on feelings of insecurity and guilt, noise, threats of violence and war, news of crime and disaster, etc. This book shows the nature of genuine psychic attacks—ranging from actual acts of black magic to bitter jealousy and hate—and the reality of psychic stress, the structure of the psyche and its interrelationship with the physical body. It shows how each person must develop his weakened aura into a powerful defense-shield, thereby gaining both physical protection and energetic well-being that can extend to protection from physical violence, accidents ... even ill health.

0-87542-190-3

288 pp., 5³⁄₁₆ x 8, illus. $9.95

Practical Guide to Psychic Powers

Awaken Your Sixth Sense

DENNING & PHILLIPS

Because you are missing out on so much without them! Who has not dreamed of possessing powers to move objects without physically touching them, to see at a distance or into the future, to know another's thoughts, to read the past of an object or person, or to find water or mineral wealth by dowsing?

This book is a complete course—teaching you step-by-step how to develop the powers that actually have been yours since birth. Psychic powers are a natural part of your mind; by expanding your mind in this way, you will gain health and vitality, emotional strength, greater success in your daily pursuits, and a new understanding of your inner self.

You'll learn to play with these new skills, working with groups of friends to accomplish things you never would have believed possible. The text shows you how to make the equipment, do the exercises—many of them at any time, anywhere—and how to use your abilities to change your life and the lives of those close to you.

0-87542-191-1
216 pp., 5³⁄₁₆ x 8, illus. $9.95

Simplified Qabala Magic

TED ANDREWS

The mystical Qabala is one of the most esoteric yet practical systems for expanding your consciousness and unfolding your spiritual gifts. Within its Tree of Life lies a map to the wisdom of the ancients, the powers of the universe and to ourselves. As the earliest form of Jewish mysticism, it is especially suited to the rational Western mind.

The Qabala has traditionally been presented as mysterious and complex. *Simplified Qabala Magic* offers a basic understanding of what the Qabala is and how it operates. It provides techniques for utilizing the forces within the system to bring peace, healing, power, love, and magic into your life.

0-7387-0394-X
192 pp., 5¼ x 8 $9.95

To Write to the Author

If you wish to contact the author or would like more information about this book, please write to the author in care of Llewellyn Worldwide and we will forward your request. Both the author and publisher appreciate hearing from you and learning of your enjoyment of this book and how it has helped you. Llewellyn Worldwide cannot guarantee that every letter written to the author can be answered, but all will be forwarded. Please write to:

Brandy Williams
⅍ Llewellyn Worldwide
P.O. Box 64383, Dept. 0-7387-0661-2
St. Paul, MN 55164-0383, U.S.A.

Please enclose a self-addressed stamped envelope for reply,
or $1.00 to cover costs. If outside U.S.A., enclose
international postal reply coupon.

Many of Llewellyn's authors have websites with additional information and resources. For more information, please visit our website at http://www.llewellyn.com.